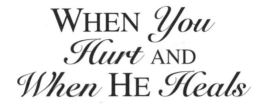

WHEN *You*
Hurt AND
When HE *Heals*

WHEN *You* *Hurt* AND *When* HE *Heals*

EXPERIENCING the SURPRISING POWER OF PRAYER

JENNIFER KENNEDY DEAN

MOODY PUBLISHERS
CHICAGO

All Scripture quotations, unless otherwise indicated, are taken from the *Holy Bible, New International Version*®. NIV®. Copyright © 1973, 1978, 1984 by International Bible Society. Used by permission of Zondervan Publishing House. All rights reserved.

Scripture quotations marked NASB are taken from the *New American Standard Bible*®, Copyright © The Lockman Foundation 1960, 1962, 1963, 1968, 1971, 1972, 1973, 1975, 1977, 1995. Used by permission.

Library of Congress Cataloging-in-Publication Data

Dean, Jennifer Kennedy.
  When you hurt and when he heals: experiencing the surprising power of prayer / Jennifer Kennedy Dean.
     p. cm.
  Includes bibliographical references.
  ISBN 0-8024-4600-0
  1. Prayer—Christianity. I. Title
  BV215.D344 2004
  248.3'2—dc22

                                    2004012475

1 3 5 7 9 10 8 6 4 2
Printed in the United States of America

To my sons:
Brantley, Kennedy, and Stinson

"And this is my prayer: that your love may abound more and more in knowledge and depth of insight, so that you may be able to discern what is best and may be pure and blameless until the day of Christ, filled with the fruit of righteousness that comes through Jesus Christ — to the glory and praise of God" (Phil. 1:9–11).

CONTENTS

Introduction   9

THE HEALER

1. Prayer's Power   17
2. God's Compassion   22
3. A Platform for His Power   26
4. Peace Like a River   31
5. Your Healer Is Your Healing   35
6. Christ in You and Christ through You   40
7. Healing Rest   44

HEALING YOUR MEMORIES

8. The Wellspring of Life   51
9. Hidden Things   56
10. His Work in You   60
11. Uproot Bitterness   67
12. Scar Tissue   73
13. Healing the Root   78

HEALING YOUR RELATIONSHIPS

14. Healing Fruit   85
15. Invitation to Wholeness   90
16. Your Freedom   95
17. Leave the Past Behind   100
18. Come into the Light   103
19. Water in the Wilderness   106

20. Progressing in Wholeness 111
21. The Finishing Touch 115
22. A Living Offering 120
23. God's Workmanship 123
24. The Surgeon's Scalpel 127
25. A New Thing 131
26. Spiritual Antioxidants 134
27. Wholeness 139

Conclusion 142

INTRODUCTION

I am convinced of this: God wants us to bring our hurts to Him in prayer. This little book consists of a series of meditations meant to encourage and challenge you to put yourself in God's hands and allow Him to begin healing you from the inside out.

I'm making no attempt to write a theological treatise on healing or argue any doctrinal position. And I want to say from the outset that I'm not writing so much for the person who has experienced deep emotional trauma. If you have wounds like these, you most likely will need deeper counsel than I can provide here. Prayer will surely be a vital part of your healing too, but God will probably put you on the way to wholeness with the help of a counselor He has gifted with wisdom for your needs.

The people I am mainly writing for are those who carry around everyday human pain, those who are stuck in limiting habits and patterns of thought and want to be set free. Maybe you find fear and anxiety ruling your emotions. Perhaps you have seen relationship after relationship poisoned by your need to control. Maybe you sense a barrier between you and others erected by your sense of inadequacy. We are all riddled with soul wounds, and if they're left to fester, their noxious impact oozes into our personalities, our relationships, our emotions, and our thought patterns. Whatever it is that holds you back and diminishes your life, I want to tell you that God desires to set you free!

My hope is that this book will nudge you into a journey on which you will open yourself to the healing balm of the Spirit of God, allowing the Healer Himself to detoxify your soul. He can speak His Word into the recesses of your heart, rooting out lies and replacing them with truth.

Through this journey, I'll have you focus your attention more on the Healer than on your hurts. Your hurtful memories and experiences will be the platform for God's power and the context for His healing work. You will examine how He can heal memories and relationships and how He can teach you to walk in wholeness.

I am neither a counselor nor a psychologist. I am a prayerful intercessor, and it's from this point of view that I wrote this book. I have seen the power of prayer accomplish what nothing else could. I started writing these meditations originally for the women for whom I was praying. I realized quickly that in praying for either physical or emotional healing, God was working at many levels. I have seen firsthand that the concepts in this little book lead people into an experience of healing power and open them to the deep work of the Spirit of God. As those for whom I was praying began to work through these meditations on a daily (or at least regular) basis, our times of prayer became much more fruitful.

These short meditations deal with healing of memories,

emotions, and relationships. But I know from experience that when the healing you need is physical, the healing of your inner person supports and activates the healing of your outer person. Scripture affirms this: "A heart at peace gives life to the body" (Prov. 14:30). I am not suggesting that all illness and disease is the result of sin or of inner wounds. I just want to say that the inner peace God has available for every one of His children will enhance the health and vitality of the body. Neither am I suggesting that inner healing of emotions and memories will automatically result in the healing of your body. But your inner wholeness will allow for a new supply of energy to be available.

For example, you may have witnessed a person who is dealing with depression or discouragement. That person is likely to be physically tired and mentally distracted. As Solomon observed, "An anxious heart weighs a man down" (Prov. 12:25). When the depression is lifted, the whole body is energized again, and thinking becomes more focused. People who have found relief for their inner pain will have a body more able to function at its optimum, fighting disease more efficiently.

Sandra D. Wilson explains in her book *Hurt People Hurt People:*

> An accumulating body of research demonstrates that our bodies and emotions are inextricably bound together in a miraculous

merger, which, of course, we know has been designed by God. This means that we wound our bodies when we wound our emotions.[1]

Another thought I want you to consider as you begin this healing journey is about how God can use the difficulties in your life if you allow Him to exercise all His power in the midst of your pain. Your hurt can be the opening for leading you into a deeper relationship with the Father. Even Job, whose suffering was never fully explained, found at the end a fuller understanding of who God is. At the end of his ordeal, we meet a new Job. Job has himself in perspective now, because he has experienced the presence of God as never before. "My ears had heard of you," he tells the Lord, "but now my eyes have seen you" (Job 42:6). Job gained something precious and irreplaceable through his ordeal. He was not diminished by his pain, but instead was enriched through his experience.

Whatever circumstances you find yourself in, and for whatever reason, I want you to feel confident that God can bring healing and maturity to you.

I don't want to imply that healing is easy and instantaneous. It's not. And it will come in the form that God chooses, which may not exactly match what you've envisioned. But I have seen healing come in response to concentrated, prolonged, persevering prayer. Praying for healing is not smooth and easy. Rarely—in my experience, never—is prayer for healing a one-time event. It takes committed prayers who don't give up when circumstances contradict their confidence.

This is what I would say to you if you and I could sit down face-to-face. This is what I have learned and pieced together over the years about how God restores from the ground up.

As you walk through this journey toward healing, I want you to keep two things in mind. First, fix your eyes more on the Healer than on your need. He is everything. He is your healing. Second, put yourself in the patient's role. That's what you are—the patient, not the doctor. Don't work hard to heal. Don't strain to recall memories. Don't try to evaluate and grade your progress. Just let God, who is truth, work in you (John 14:6; 1 John 5:6).

ᗆ—HOW TO USE THIS BOOK

I have divided this book into four sections. The first section lays the foundation for healing. It challenges you to fix your eyes on your Healer. It encourages you to be open to whatever He wants to do in you. The second section deals with healing of memories or personal healing. You will find that most other layers of woundedness have their roots in hurtful memories that have laid a false foundation for understanding yourself, love, and relationships. The third section deals with healing of relationships, and the fourth section gives guidance for living in wholeness and freedom. Each section has short meditations and includes reflective questions.

The arrangement of the book lends itself easily to a small group experience as well as individual reflection. You may want to spend more than one day on each meditation. Please use it any way that best meets your needs.

If you use this book with a prayer partner or a prayer group, I think you will find that these concepts will redefine your prayer experience together and give you a deep focus for your group praying. The elements of healing that begin to unfold in your life may be strengthened and furthered as you work through them with a group of like-minded believers.

Finally, as you read this book, I will be praying that the Spirit of truth will disclose to you the power of your Healer.

1. Sandra D. Wilson, *Hurt People Hurt People* (Uhrichsville, Ohio: Discovery House Publishers, 2001), 111.

The Healer

PRAYER'S POWER

May God himself, the God of peace, sanctify you through and through. May your whole spirit, soul and body be kept blameless at the coming of our Lord Jesus Christ. The one who calls you is faithful and he will do it (1 Thess. 5:23–24).

Prayer is a conduit through which the power of God flows. Prayer brings the power of heaven into the circumstances of earth. God has designed prayer to be the avenue by which the power promised in Scripture becomes available to His people.

If we take God at His Word, then nothing on earth is beyond the reach of His astounding power. "Ah, Sovereign LORD, you have made the heavens and the earth by your great power and outstretched arm. Nothing is too hard for you" (Jer. 32:17).

Am I overusing the word *power?* My writer's instincts tell me I am. But there is no other word to take its place. Power is the essence of prayer. James 5:16 states: "The prayer of a righteous man is powerful and effective." Prayer is not a benign, feel-good, stress-relieving exercise. Prayer releases the power of God to change the circumstances of earth.

In this book, we will consider specifically the power of prayer to bring healing. As we examine what the Word of God tells us about this topic, keep in mind that prayer is not convincing God or even bringing your need to His attention. He knows what you will need before you need it; He yearns to supply your need and is awakening in you the inclination to seek Him and His provision. Prayer is simply opening your life to receive what He has to give.

Ole Hallesby, one of Norway's leading Christian teachers, wrote, "To pray is nothing more involved than to let Jesus into our needs. To pray is to give Jesus permission to employ His powers in the alleviation of our distress. . . . To pray is nothing more involved than to open the door, giving Jesus access to our needs and permitting Him to exercise His own power in dealing with them."[2] And E. Stanley Jones writes in *Abundant Living,* "Prayer is . . . the opening of a channel from your emptiness to God's fullness."[3]

Whatever form of healing you need, God is able to do it. God cares about every aspect of your being. He created you to be a multidimensional creature, one layer interacting with and affecting another layer. In 1 Thessalonians 5:23, Paul prays that "your whole spirit, soul and body be kept blameless." John writes to his friend Gaius, "Beloved, I pray that in all respects you may prosper and be in good health, just as your soul prospers" (3 John 2 NASB). "*In all respects,*" he says. And he uses the word prosper, a Greek word that means "to be led down a good path" or "succeed."[4] Every part of you—your spirit, your soul, and your body—matter to God. He created all of you.

Your Creator does not disregard any part of you. You may begin these days with one agenda for healing, only to discover that the need extends to another level. You may begin with a felt need for healing a relationship, only to discover that first you need a healing in your memories.

My friend Anna wanted prayer because she had done all she could do to repair her failing marriage. Her husband seemed oblivious to the fact that she was miserable. She felt continually angry with him, and that anger seemed to grow with each new offense. And the offenses seemed to come daily.

As we prayed regularly together, I asked Anna to concentrate on taking her focus off of what her husband did to hurt her and instead to observe what these hurtful incidents made her feel—other than angry. She found that as she monitored her emotional responses, a pattern emerged. At the bottom of most of her hurt feelings was a sense of having failed. She knew that her mother had regularly communicated to her that nothing she did was ever good enough. In subtle ways her mother caused Anna to feel as if her decisions were wrong and her actions never measured up to her mother's expectations.

Anna began to realize that she read into her husband's words what she was used to hearing from her mother. This realization led her to deeper inner healing as she came to a compassionate understanding of her mother. Anna also recognized that she believed that she was a failure and expected to hear it from others. Her need for healing in a relationship was the impetus for a deeper healing.

So be open to how the Spirit directs your thoughts, and

trust Him. Know that He can and will guide you into all truth. "The lamp of the LORD searches the spirit of a man; it searches out his inmost being" (Prov. 20:27). "You will know the truth, and the truth will set you free" (John 8:32).

Are you willing right now to open your entire life to His healing presence? Even knowing that His power may interrupt cherished sin-patterns or challenge comfortable beliefs? Do you want *all of Him* more than you want any other thing? You can have as much of Him that you make room for.

⌒—REFLECT

As you begin this healing journey, what is motivating you to seek the Healer? List your symptoms as you perceive them right now.

Do you have any anxiety about putting yourself in the hands of the Healer and holding nothing back? Are there areas of your life that you would like to keep off-limits from Him? Remember, you can be fearlessly honest. He knows your heart inside and out. Write out today's date, and give a brief description of the circumstances of your life right now. This will be a reference point for you for years to come.

⌒—PRAYER

Lord, I am opening myself fully to You. I release all of my needs to You. I invite You to search out the hidden toxins in my soul. I want to cooperate with You in the healing You will bring. Let the rushing, mighty wind of Your Spirit blow through my life. Even now I thank You for the mighty and powerful work of healing You have already begun and will complete. I claim it now as my own. Amen.

HEAR HIS HEART

"Being confident of this, that he who began a good work in you will carry it on to completion until the day of Christ Jesus" (Phil. 1:6).

GOD'S COMPASSION

Filled with compassion, Jesus reached out his hand and touched the man. "I am willing," he said. "Be clean!" (Mark 1:41).

God is full of compassion. The word compassion actually means "to suffer with" (com, "with"; pati, "to suffer, bear"). To say that God has compassion on you means that your pain, your need, touches His heart as if it were His own.

Are there people in your life whom you love so deeply and with whom you are so intimately connected that their pain hurts you more than your own? Truthfully, I have more difficulty recovering from my children's hurts than from my own. Their pain is more painful to me than it is to them sometimes. But hurting with them and for them is usually all I can do. My compassion for them does not heal them. So it is wonderful to know that God also has compassion on them.

God's compassion compels Him to exercise His power on our behalf. The Lord defines His compassion this way: "Can a mother forget the baby at her breast and have no compassion on the child she has borne? Though she may forget, I will not forget you! See, I have engraved you on the palms of my hands" (Isa. 49:15–16).

In this word-picture, Isaiah is setting up a highly unlikely, almost impossible scenario: *Could a mother forget her nursing child?* He used the same device in a later chapter: "'Though the mountains be shaken and the hills be removed, yet my unfailing love for you will not be shaken nor my covenant of peace be removed,' says the LORD, who has compassion on you" (54:10). Here's the logic: As impossible as this scenario is, what God is proclaiming is *even more* impossible. Even if a mother could forget her nursing child, God says that He would never, never forget you.

Why is it so impossible for a mother to forget her nursing child? When a nursing baby cries, the mother's body is suddenly flooded with what the baby needs. It is an amazing physiological phenomenon that the cry of need releases the supply. When a woman's body is full of the baby's provision, the mother is in pain until the baby nurses—takes what she has ready to give. The cry of hunger is met with an answering cry of compassion. She cannot forget her nursing child because her body reminds her.

Like the nursing mother, God is completely sufficient to provide what you need, and He has the supreme power to deliver it.

Even more wonderful than that, your pain echoes in His heart. And He is so full of provision that He aches for you to receive it from Him. He knows about the need before you do, and the supply is ready and waiting for you. He hears your cry before it escapes your lips—while it is still an inarticulate groaning to which you have not attached words. Never at any moment is your pain or your need silent before Him. Even when you are not consciously thinking of it or feeling it, He sees it and knows it. As the psalmist wrote, "All my longings lie open before you, O Lord; my sighing is not hidden from you" (Ps. 38:9).

It is not the cry of the lips but the cry of the heart that God hears. "Before they call I will answer; while they are still speaking I will hear" (Isa. 65:24).

❧—REFLECT

Describe compassion as you have felt it for another person. Often an element in human compassion is the sense of helplessness. Was that part of your experience? Describe how that felt.

Write a statement about the confidence you have in God, even if you cannot define what you need.

❧—PRAYER

Lord Almighty—El Shaddai—I believe that You Yourself are the answer to my heart's cry. I need You because You are full and overflowing with the power to heal me. I am coming to You now, receiving Your compassion. Let your power flow over me, through me, in me. Amen.

HEAR HIS HEART

"Let your face shine on your servant; save me in your unfailing love" (Ps. 31:16).

A PLATFORM FOR HIS POWER

All things are yours, whether Paul or Apollos or Cephas or the
world or life or death or the present or the future—all are yours,
and you are of Christ, and Christ is of God (1 Cor. 3:21–23).

To know firsthand God's compassion, to receive into
your experience His life-giving power, all you need to do is
turn your need toward Him. Let your need for healing—
whether it be a need for emotional healing, healing of memories,
healing of a relationship, or physical healing—be the platform
for His power.

Do you doubt that He could be full of compassion for
you? Have you believed that you are not valuable enough to
Him that He should long to care for your needs? Do you rehearse your failures and your shortcomings and convince
yourself that He could not possibly yearn over you and ache to
give you every good thing? Do you see Him as maintaining
distance between Himself and you—as if He holds Himself
aloof and shuns you?

Look at the end of God's very own definition of His compassion: "See, I have engraved you on the palms of my hands"
(Isa. 49:16). Just as His people write on their hands "The
Lord's" as a sign of their belonging to and reverence for Him
(44:5), so God Himself carves on His hands His belonging and
eternal attentiveness to His people.

What else does an engraving or carving on God's palms

remind you of? Yes, the nail-scarred hands of Jesus. Do you see? The stakes that were meant for your hands pierced His instead. The whip that was meant for your back fell on His instead. The scorn meant for you He took. The unimaginably savage death you deserved He bore for you. All for you! All for you! His compassion for you is no sentimental, imaginary feeling. It caused Him to step into your place and let your punishment be inflicted upon Him (see Isa. 52:13–53:12).

My dear friend, would He pay the full price for you and then withhold from you any good thing? The remedy to every pain or grief or difficulty that comes into your life was provided for in His death and resurrection. Does He not want you to have everything He paid so high a price to obtain? Paul assures us that "He who did not spare his own Son, but gave him up for us all—how will he not also, along with him, graciously give us all things?" (Rom. 8:32).

Imagine that someone purchased an appliance for you and also paid for a warranty to take care of any repairs. Imagine that at some point the appliance breaks down and is in need of repair. You don't know about the warranty, so you forgo the use of your appliance because you can't afford the repair. Then imagine the giver's despair when she discovers that you have not accessed the provision she had already paid for. Think of her sorrow at knowing that you have scraped by when she had already paid the price that would guarantee you exactly what you needed.

God, too, has paid for your healing. He has paid for your wholeness. He wants you to have the fullness of everything that is already yours in Him. Paul writes in 1 Corinthians 3:21 that "all things are yours." Why? Because you belong to Christ, and Christ belongs to God. You belong to Christ because He has purchased you. Now everything He has is yours, and He has everything because He is God's.

He is so determined that you should have everything He paid for that He put His life in you as a guarantee (Eph. 1:13–14). His love for you is so intense that it compels Him to come near. He desires intimacy with you to such an extent that He has made His home with you (John 14:23). He is not a faraway, arms-length, distant deity. Turn to Him, and you will find rest for your soul.

Take to heart the words of Major Ian Thomas:

If you are to know the fulness of life in Christ, you are to appropriate the efficacy of what He is. . . . Relate everything, moment by moment as it arises, to the adequacy of what He is in you, and assume that His adequacy will be operative. . . . Simply expose by faith every situation as it arises, to the allsufficiency of the One who indwells you by His life. Can any situation possibly arise, in any circumstances, for which He is not adequate? Any pressure, promise, problem, responsibility or temptation for which the Lord Jesus Himself is not adequate? If He be truly God, there cannot be a single one![5]

REFLECT

Do you think there is anything—any problem, any hurt, any illness—for which Christ is inadequate? Is He lacking anything?

In his tender poem to love, Solomon has the bride declare to her bridegroom, "My beloved is mine, and I am his" (Song 2:16 NASB). As the bride of Christ, you belong to Jesus, and Jesus belongs to you. Everything He is belongs to you, and everything you are belongs to Him. What does that mean to you?

PRAYER

Lord, I do want all that You have provided for me. I do not want to miss out on Your abundance. I choose to believe Your Word—that You love me with an everlasting love, that nothing will keep the full force of Your love from me. I welcome Your love into my life and my circumstances. You love me. You love me. You love me. Amen, and amen.

HEAR HIS HEART

Who shall separate us from the love of Christ? Shall trouble or hardship or persecution or famine or nakedness or danger or sword? . . . No, in all these things we are more than conquerors through him who loved us. For I am convinced that neither death nor

*life, neither angels nor demons, neither the present
nor the future, nor any powers, neither height nor
depth, nor anything else in all creation, will be able
to separate us from the love of God that is in Christ
Jesus our Lord (Rom. 8:35, 37–39).*

PEACE LIKE A RIVER

*"If only you had paid attention to my commands, your
peace would have been like a river" (Isa. 48:18).*

The salvation for which Christ died is a complete salvation. The word translated "salvation" (the root is the Greek word *sozo*) also has as one of its meanings "to heal." Jesus is interested in your mind, in your emotions, in your relationships, in your memories, in your body, in everything about you. Whatever hurts you matters to Him.

He cares about your wholeness. Once you begin to open your life to His power and provision, He will leave no part of you unchanged. Real prayer leaves nothing untouched. He will push through the barriers you have erected and penetrate areas you want to leave alone. All because He loves you. All because He is not willing to compromise your wholeness.

Do you hear His voice right now speaking in your heart— "Would you be made whole?" What is your response? Perhaps you need to consider what it means to be made whole before you can respond honestly.

You are made up of many arenas. You have the faculty to think and reason, to feel, to remember, to love. All of who you are is packaged in a body. Your body is your vehicle for relating to the material realm—the physical environment in which you live. God's goal for you is that all your parts would work together as one integrated whole. His desire for you is that all of you would be in tandem, operating in unity.

Sin brought disunity, not only between God and humans, but also within each human. In our fallen state, each of us is in conflict with ourselves. The human experience became this: "I do not understand what I do. For what I want to do I do not do, but what I hate I do" (Rom. 7:15).

Do you experience conflict with yourself? Do you believe one way and act another? Do your emotions rule your thoughts even when they contradict what your mind believes? Is your spirit willing but your flesh weak (Matt. 26:41)? Do you long for the conflict to end? Do you want the peace that wholeness brings?

At the moment of salvation, God in all His fullness comes to indwell your spirit. Your spirit is justified, freed, made right with God. As Paul wrote to the Corinthian church, "He who unites himself with the Lord is one with him in spirit" (1 Cor. 6:17). From that moment, He is in the process of restoring your soul (mind, will, and emotions—your human nature) to its intended purpose—to be the place where He communes with you and displays His glory.

God comes into your life and begins to make Himself known as Jehovah Rapha, "the Lord Your Healing." The Hebrew word *rapha* has as one of its meanings "to mend by stitching; to make whole." So think of the Lord as "stitching" together the various aspects of your nature, making them parts of one whole, lining up your personality and your body to work in harmony with His Life in your spirit.

As that occurs—as you begin to respond to His life in you—you find that peace flows through you. The layers of your nature are working together productively instead of sabotaging each other. His peace reigns in you, guarding and watching over your heart. "And the peace of God, which transcends all understanding, will guard your hearts and your minds in Christ Jesus" (Phil. 4:7). Jesus promises you His peace. Not peace as the world knows it, not peace that is determined by outward circumstances, but peace within (see John 14:27).

No layer is isolated from the others. All are intertwined. You may experience your need for healing, for example, in a relationship. This may be what you come to the Healer for. As you respond to Him in obedience, His peace and His healing power begin to flow through you like a river. You will find it working in your emotions, in your memories, in your physical being. His power takes its own path. Will you follow Him on that path?

ᎧᲘ REFLECT

In what ways do you experience conflict between the different aspects of your nature? How does this inner conflict spill out to those around you, causing conflict in your experience?

☙—PRAYER

Jehovah Rapha, I celebrate Your healing presence in me. I know that You can still the turmoil within me. I know that You can bring wholeness to my mind, will, and emotions. I know that You, gentle Healer, love me and have only my welfare in mind. I trust You. Let the river flow. Amen.

HEAR HIS HEART

"Peace I leave with you; my peace I give you. I do not give to you as the world gives. Do not let your hearts be troubled and do not be afraid" (John 14:27).

❧

YOUR HEALER IS YOUR HEALING

"On that day a fountain will be opened to the house of David and the inhabitants of Jerusalem, to cleanse them from sin and impurity" (Zech. 13:1).

Once Jesus Christ has become Lord of your life and has come to indwell your spirit, you're made forever whole. He is your healing. Now begins the process of entering into your salvation more fully, with every part of your being.

As you set out now to experience His healing and His wholeness, get this fixed in your mind: your healing is within you. God is your healing, and His Spirit is in you. F. B. Meyer called Him "the living Fountain rising up in the well of our personality."[6] By cooperating with His healing power, you are surrendering yourself in deeper and more meaningful ways to His lordship. Opening your life to His presence is opening your life to His healing. His healing does not come separately from Himself.

His healing presence begins to permeate your mind, your will, and your emotions. The wholeness of your spirit will then spread, infusing your personality with His power—a process similar to the yeast that leavens the whole loaf. Or to use another image, the healing that rises up as a fountain in you spills over even in the very cells of your body. Healing rejuvenates your mind, your memories, your instinctive responses, your emotions, your perceptions, and your body.

The healing God pours out in you will go deep. It will soak into your soul and saturate your mind. In the book of Hebrews we read,

> *For the word of God is living and active. Sharper than any double-edged sword, it penetrates even to dividing soul and spirit, joints and marrow; it judges the thoughts and attitudes of the heart. Nothing in all creation is hidden from God's sight. Everything is uncovered and laid bare before the eyes of him to whom we must give account (Heb. 4:12–13).*

This might have called to mind for the writer's Jewish audience the role of the priest in examining animals to determine their fitness as sacrifices, since the sacrifice had to be pure, spotless, and without blemish. The priest would examine the skin, then the muscle layer, then the organs, and finally the bones and the bone marrow, each layer laid open by the priest's double-edged knife. Even if everything else looked spotless, there might be something in the bone marrow. Something that had not yet manifested itself in any other portion of the body but would eventually find its way from the bone marrow into the bloodstream and into the organs of the body. Do you see how deep the examination went?

You, my friend, are not being examined to see if you are presentable. Your sacrifice—the precious Lamb of God—has already been examined, and no fault or blemish has been found in Him. But the word of God is penetrating with its life and energy into the marrow of your soul to bring healing at the deepest levels—even finding and healing the festering memories of which you have no conscious recollection.

David Seamands, in his book *Redeeming the Past,* explains:

Many of us have hurtful memories which we try to push out of our minds. Such memories cannot be healed by the mere passage of time any more than an infected wound could be. The infection turns inward and actually worsens because it spreads to other areas, affecting and infecting them. So it is with certain painful experiences, especially those that happened during the important years of early childhood and teenage development.[7]

Nothing can hide from God's healing power. All of it is laid bare before Him. Even hurts that lie so deeply buried that you cannot state them in words. These, too, are open before Him. "Before a word is on my tongue you know it completely, O LORD" (Ps. 139:4). "All my longings lie open before you, O LORD; my sighing is not hidden from you" (Ps. 38:9).

This healing is not something you have to "get." Healing is yours. The Holy Spirit is a fountain of healing in you. He is the Word of God spoken into the depths of your soul, bringing order and light.

Paul prays that you will "be kept blameless," in your "spirit, soul and body" (1 Thess. 5:23). Wholeness is when your whole being is functioning as an integrated whole. So bring all of yourself to God. Abandon yourself completely to His power-filled presence. Let Him well up in you, filling and saturating you with all of Himself.

ᴓ—REFLECT

Think about the accounts in the Gospels of Jesus healing people. Choose a story. Close your eyes and use your sanctified imagination to put yourself into the role of the person Jesus healed. Imagine with all your senses.

Is Jesus any less able to heal you?

Is Jesus any less willing to heal you?

Isn't it true that Jesus is even nearer to you than He was to the person in the Gospel account? He was with them, but He is in you.

ᴓ—PRAYER

Healing Jesus, well up in me. Leave no part of me unchanged. Do everything that needs to be done. Be healing in me. Amen.

HEAR HIS HEART

"The LORD will guide you always;
he will satisfy your needs in a sun-scorched land
and will strengthen your frame.
You will be like a well-watered garden,
like a spring whose waters never fail" (Isa. 58:11).

CHRIST IN YOU AND CHRIST THROUGH YOU

*"Now that I, your Lord and Teacher, have washed your feet,
you also should wash one another's feet" (John 13:14).*

Is it selfish or self-centered to desire wholeness for yourself? Would your time and effort not be better spent reaching out to others? Isn't it a sign of spiritual immaturity to focus on your own needs?

Dear friend, please reject the sense of insignificance that tells you that you should ignore your needs and that you are only valuable for what you can do for others. That is entirely false.

I want you to relax. You will find that as healing flows through you, it also flows *from* you. As Christ restores you, you will become a vessel for His healing, carrying it into the lives of others. True healing will not make you self-absorbed. Instead it will free you to be a willing, eager servant to those in need around you.

Remember Jesus' words? "Now that I, your Lord and Teacher, have washed your feet, you also should wash one another's feet. I have set you an example that you should do as I have done for you" (John 13:14–15). You cannot wash the feet of others until He has washed your feet. Once you have personally experienced His love for you, then you are called to show that very same love to those around you.

Often the serving we do is out of our own neediness instead

of our wholeness. It is possible to serve others in order to control them, attempting to manage our environment and try to make it meet our need to feel whole. When we are wounded inside, we tend to look for peace and happiness outside. External circumstances become the focus. If we can keep our circumstances under control, if we can surround ourselves with possessions and relationships and situations that make us feel significant, then maybe happiness is possible. If we can take care of other people and solve their problems for them, we can ensure that they value us. The problem is that the externals will not stay in order. You will be caught in a trap. Your work will never be done. It will wear you out.

Your wounds, your anxieties, your bitterness compel you to respond to others in certain ways. Some of these responses are disguised as loving, and you mean them to be loving. Others are blatantly harsh or unkind, and you seem unable consistently to rein them in. In either case, your responses are originating in the wounded areas of your soul rather than from the wholeness of your spirit, the indwelling life of Christ. Your healing and wholeness is the key to ministering to others. It is from the places where you have been wounded and have experienced—or are experiencing—the healing that only Christ can bring that His life flows like a river of living water. Allowing Christ to well up in you, bringing His healing to you, is one of the most loving and serving actions you can take for those around you.

Christ in you wants to flow through you unhindered, dispensing His life to all with whom you come into contact. Let Him wash your feet, then you wash the feet of those around you. Let Him meet your needs, then you will be free to meet the needs of others. Once your wounds have experienced His healing touch, they will be the strength from which you serve others.

⌒—REFLECT

Do you see any responses emanating from your own hurts and insecurities that masquerade as service to others? Might you be serving others from a desire for their approval rather than out of your personal encounter with Jesus?

How do you feel about the idea that as you experience marrow-deep healing, the shape of those responses might change?

Are you willing to let them go?

⌒—PRAYER

My Lord, I release all my external circumstances to You. I commit to You that I will stop manipulating situations. I will stop trying to control people. I will trust You with all the outer trappings and I will fix my eyes on You in me. Live fully in me, Jesus. Draw me to You. Fasten my heart on You. Amen.

HEAR HIS HEART

"Praise be to the God and Father of our Lord Jesus Christ, the Father of compassion and the God of all comfort, who comforts us in all our troubles, so that we can comfort those in any trouble with the comfort we ourselves have received from God" (2 Cor. 1:3–4).

HEALING REST
"Be still, and know that I am God" (Ps. 46:10).

What kind of healing do you need? No matter the kind, God is as able to heal your memories as He is to heal your body. He is as able to heal your sin-patterns as He is to heal your relationships. He is not at all overwhelmed by your need for healing. It is all within His scope and well within His ability. He knows exactly how to diagnose your illness and precisely how to treat it. He has established a protocol for healing that He designed just for you, targeting your need and working within the framework of your personality and experiences.

You belong to Him. He has called you by name. Before you were born, He marked out a path for you. He knit you together in your mother's womb. He has your days written in His book. He knows you inside and out. He knows your thoughts before you speak them. He understands your sighs. There is nothing about you He does not fully know and understand (Ps. 139). Whatever you need to know, He can tell you. "He reveals deep and hidden things; he knows what lies in darkness, and light dwells with him" (Dan. 2:22).

If you will, please turn your thoughts to a woman we meet in Mark 5:25–34. Her body had become her enemy. For twelve years her body had been bleeding, and no one could make it stop. "She had suffered a great deal under the care of many doctors and had spent all she had, yet instead of getting better she grew worse" (v. 26). No one could diagnose her. No one understood her ailment.

As her body was damaged by disease, her soul was damaged by rejection and shame. The wounds that had been inflicted on her emotions were the most devastating of all. The nature of her illness, a twelve-year-long menstrual flow, marked her as "unclean." Anyone who bumped up against her became ritually defiled and had to perform the rites of cleansing. Can you imagine how many times in the course of her illness she had been demeaned and humiliated as her inconvenient presence interrupted someone's day?

Then, one day, she touched Jesus. Just the hem of His outer robe—not a bold enough touch to be noticed, she thought. She could get by with just touching His garment. "She came up behind him in the crowd and touched his cloak" (v. 27). And the most astounding thing happened. The life in Him flowed into her. The life in Him overcame the death in her. "Immediately her bleeding stopped and she felt in her body that she was freed from her suffering" (v. 29). But her elation turned to fear when He asked, "Who touched my clothes?"

She had learned the skill of being invisible. She found safety in hiding. She had so carefully planned her approach—she would sneak up behind Him in the crowd and just touch His clothes, not His person. But here He was, calling her front and center. She tried to disappear into the crowd, but she found that she could not hide from Him. "Jesus kept looking around to see who had done it. Then the woman, knowing what had happened to her, came and fell at his feet and, trembling with fear, told him the whole truth" (vv. 32–33).

She braced herself for the scorn she knew was coming. Yet she found instead that Jesus looked her in the eyes and called her by a new name: "*Daughter,* your faith has healed you. Go in peace and be freed from your suffering" (v. 34, emphasis added).

You see, He was not satisfied just to heal her body. He wanted to heal her soul. When the healing flooded her body, she had what she desired from Him. But He did not have what He desired from her. He longed to bring her into His presence where He could shower her with love. He wanted to make her whole.

She did not need another diagnosis. She did not need another name for her disease. She did not need another explanation of her symptoms. She needed to touch Jesus. And we need to touch Him too.

Not only does Jesus fully know and understand you, He also knows and fully understands that what ails you—whether emotional or physical. He knows your wounded emotions and your painful memories better than you do.

Are your doctors stymied by your symptoms? Are you mystified by the source of your emotional pain? Are you out of ideas for how to help your wounded relationships?

Turn to Jesus—reach out and touch Him. He knows all that you need.

Let it rest with Him. You can safely leave it all in His hands. He will not fail you. Enter into the soul-sabbath that absolute faith in Him makes possible. Rest.

"None ever sought Me in vain. I wait, wait, with a hungry longing to be called upon; and I, who have already seen your hearts' needs before you cried upon Me, perhaps before you were conscious of those needs yourself, I am already preparing the answer."[8]

ᴑ—REFLECT

List the things that puzzle you or cause you to feel anxious and uncertain. As you list each thing, let it be an act of placing it on the altar and leaving it in His hands.

ᴑ—PRAYER

Lord, please heal me. I trust You. I look to You. You are the artist and I am Your masterpiece. Create of me what You will. I am Yours. Amen.

HEAR HIS HEART

"I went down to the potter's house, and I saw him
working at the wheel. But the pot he was shaping
from the clay was marred in his hands; so the
potter formed it into another pot, shaping
it as seemed best to him" (Jer. 18:3–4).

2. O. Hallesby, *Prayer* (Minneapolis: Augsburg Publishing House, 1931), 12.

3. E. Stanley Jones, *Abundant Living* (Nashville: Abingdon Press, 1942), 16.

4. Andrew E. Hill, "Prosper; Prosperous," in *The International Standard Bible Encyclopedia*, rev. ed. (Grand Rapids: William B. Eerdmans Publishing Co., 1986), vol. 3, 1012.

5. Major Ian Thomas, *The Saving Life* (Grand Rapids: Zondervan, 1961), 18.

6. F. B. Meyer, *Our Daily Walk* (Grand Rapids: Zondervan 1989), 169.

7. David A Seamands, *Redeeming the Past* (Colorado Springs, Colo.: Victor Books, 2002), 37.

8. A. J. Russell, ed., *God Calling*, by Two Listeners (New York: Jove Books, 1993), 28.

· · · · · · · · · · · · · · · · · ∞ · · · · · · · · · · · · · · · · · ·

SECTION TWO

Healing Your Memories

❧

THE WELLSPRING OF LIFE

Above all else, guard your heart, for it is the wellspring of life
(Prov. 4:23).

The Hebrew word translated *heart* could accurately be rendered "mind." It is the center of thought, reasoning, and emotion. So your mind is the wellspring of life. A wellspring is "a source of continual supply."[9] All of your reactions, responses, and emotions flow from your heart and mind. If the source, the wellspring, is contaminated, everything that flows from it will be too. As Jesus said, "The good man brings good things out of the good stored up in him, and the evil man brings evil things out of the evil stored up in him" (Matt. 12:35).

Your mind organizes information and experiences and assigns meaning to them. It files them for you and gives them labels. It also compares new input and experiences to existing files and cross-references them so that old thoughts, feelings, beliefs, and experiences help define new ones. In this way, new experiences are automatically linked to old ones.

Because of the way your mind works, something that enters your experience today will very likely evoke emotions associated with experiences from the past. This is so ingrained that the process goes unnoticed. It feels to you like a response to the present moment, but it is really a cumulative response from cross-referenced experiences throughout your life.

If, for example, early in your life you had numerous experiences that your mind labeled "rejection," those files are filled with self-loathing. The meaning your mind assigned was "I'm unlovable. I'm not good enough. I'm incompetent." Later, as new files were added, you began to have files labeled "anger," "defensiveness," "need to prove my worth," "need to be right." Keep in mind that all these files are linked and cross-referenced. Every new experience and interaction is defined by the beliefs already on file.

So you interpret most experiences as rejection, either overt or subtle. That activates the self-loathing file, which activates the defensiveness file, which activates the anger file, which activates the need to be right file. On a computer, when you open one file, all the files linked to it automatically open. And so it is with your mind's filing system. You can't open one file without all linked files opening with it.

A friend of mine grew up in squalid poverty. Her early days were filled with shame and embarrassment. She was looked down on and scorned. Today she is a beautiful and accomplished woman. She was, however, extremely defensive when anyone tried to correct her or even make a suggestion to her. She read criticism into many comments that were not even slightly critical. She felt compelled to cover over any small mistake she might make by lying about it.

Before she began to seek inner healing through prolonged prayer, her reactions seemed justified to her. But gradually she realized she was assuming that anyone who knew the "real her" would look down on her and reject her. She feared that any slipping of her façade would show that little, barefoot, dirty girl she once was.

As she healed, she became aware of her reactions. "When I felt all those defensive and shame files opening, I'd step back from the moment mentally and spiritually. I asked the Spirit to show me truth. I intentionally lined my reactions up with truth. After years of practice, the truth is now my truth."

The power of the living God can refile and redefine your past experiences, bringing healing to memories that have been coloring your present experiences. He will not change the past, but He will allow you to see the past through His eyes. You can revisit those old, hurtful experiences, and with the Holy Spirit as your loving guide, you can "extract the precious from the worthless" (Jer. 15:19, NASB). For example, you can see the things that have added wisdom or compassion or dependence on God that could have come in no other way. You can see the ways that God was present, protecting you from the full force of your experience.

Norman Wright explains in his book *Making Peace with Your Past:* "A painful memory can become a healed gift instead of a searing reminder. How does this healing occur? By facing your memories, remembering them, letting them out of their closet." [10]

In that old memory, you might also recognize a lie that you embraced about yourself or about God. When you identify those lies that have worked themselves into the fabric of your life and have poisoned your wellspring, you then have the freedom to deliberately and willfully reject them. You can start the process of replacing them with the truth that sets you free.

ᕙ—REFLECT

I want to remind you again: Do not work and strain to recall memories. Instead let the Holy Spirit bring to me surface what is necessary. Why do I feel so strongly about this? Because the memories that occur to you might not be in the distant past. They might be recent memories. What I believe the Holy Spirit will guide you to are those events in your life that still cause you pain when you remember them. And please know that you don't have to complete this process in a day. In fact, you can't. You will go through this process again and again throughout your life.

Recognize that Jesus is going to be in you and with you as you remember. With a strong awareness of His presence, let the memory surface. See it unfold as you rest safely in the protective and loving embrace of Jesus.

Let Him point out to you the lie you believed about yourself. Let Him tell you the truth.

Let Him point out to you any lies you might have believed about the person who hurt you. Let Him tell you the truth.

Let Him tell you the productive things that were added to you through this experience, even though it was hurtful. Let Him tell you the truth.

Eventually you'll be able to listen to Him as He tells you that He forgives your offender and has already died for that sin. And when that time comes, you can let Him forgive through you.

ᕊ—PRAYER

Master, Savior, Healer, renew the spirit of my mind. Put Your thoughts in me. I give You every past hurt. You know each one better than I do. Bring light and freedom to my mind. Clean all the untruth out of my memory files. I look to You. Amen.

HEAR HIS HEART

"Test me, O LORD, and try me, examine my heart and my mind; for your love is ever before me, and I walk continually in your truth" (Ps. 26:2–3).

Hidden Things

"He reveals deep and hidden things;
he knows what lies in darkness,
and light dwells with him" (Dan. 2:22).

Many of the experiences that color your present may not be things that you consciously recall. Several things can account for this. Let's examine one today and another in our next reflection.

Your mind, at its subconscious level, is like a magnet. Everything sticks to it. Every impression, every experience, every emotion is banked in your subconscious mind. These stored memories and impressions actively shape your perceptions in the present. Every experience you have today will be filtered through a paradigm that your subconscious mind has constructed over your lifetime. You will respond to today in light of all your yesterdays, dating back to impressions made even in the womb.

Recent research strongly suggests that babies in the womb respond to sounds and emotions and retain memories. So you are unaware of many of the occurrences that dictate your reactions and perceptions today. Some of these impressions became embedded in your emotional memory from the time when the universe of your mind consisted only of sensation and imagery. You had no logic or ability to evaluate or reason. Yet they are part of you forever.

The part of your brain that activates factual memory—memory of events—is called the hippocampus. The part that activates emotional memory—the stored emotion from an event—is called the amygdala. The hippocampus is not fully developed before the age of three, but the amygdala is present from the time you are a fetus. Therefore, your brain may have stored an emotional memory, but your brain has no factual memory to go with it. [11]

Many of your memories are recorded only as impressions and emotions. You don't consciously remember the event. This gives the impressions more power, because to you it's something you "just know." It doesn't seem to have come from a skewed view of an event, because you don't remember the event. Only the emotion lives in your mind.

But the Father, who knit you together in your mother's womb, knows. You can ask Him to bring healing into your earliest, precognitive memories. You can invite Him into your emotional memory to do a deep work that He alone can do. He can remove the toxins from those memories and leave them powerless. Remember you don't have to consciously remember an event to ask the Spirit, who searches the deep and hidden things, to heal.

David Seamands writes of his experience with this:

Again and again I have been amazed at the power which painful memories from infancy seem to have in adult experience.

Years ago when I first began the ministry of inner healing, I was very skeptical of these early memories. Slowly but surely, I have been forced to abandon my skepticism and in several instances have had to pray for the healing of memories which could only have begun before birth.[12]

Your role in this healing is to keep your attention on God. Worship Him. Adore Him. Follow Him. All the while, He is performing a sort of spiritual chemotherapy in you. He is directing healing power to cancerous memories and emotions, destroying their power to continue hurting you. He is bringing truth to your inner parts. As the psalmist reminds us, "Surely you desire truth in the inner parts; you teach me wisdom in the inmost place" (Ps. 51:6). Let Him do His work.

ᥫ—REFLECT

Prayerfully read through these verses from Psalm 139.

For you created my inmost being;
you knit me together in my mother's womb.
I praise you because I am fearfully and wonderfully made;
your works are wonderful,
I know that full well.
My frame was not hidden from you
when I was made in the secret place.

When I was woven together in the depths of the earth,
your eyes saw my unformed body.
All the days ordained for me
were written in your book
before one of them came to be (vv. 13–16).

Write out what the Holy Spirit is speaking to you from this
passage.

Spend time worshiping the Lord, focusing on His presence,
knowing that He is performing a healing at depths you cannot
know.

⌁—PRAYER

Creator, Sustainer. Move over the surface of my mind. Search
out the hidden memories. Command them to release their toxins.
Let the cleansing power of Your life in me scrub my memories
clean of all their poisonous and hurtful power. Amen.

HEAR HIS HEART

Search me, O God, and know my heart;
test me and know my anxious thoughts.
See if there is any offensive way in me,
and lead me in the way everlasting (Ps. 139:23–24).

HIS WORK IN YOU

"I know that you can do all things;
no plan of yours can be thwarted" (Job 42:2).

Your unawareness of experiences that color your present-day perceptions and reactions might also be caused by the conscious mind's ability to bury painful memories. Sometimes events or circumstances are too much for you to deal with at the time, so as a protective defense, your mind sets the memories aside. Perhaps you can cope with it better later, or perhaps your subconscious will try to push it down forever. When a memory pathway goes unused for a period of time, your brain prunes it and puts it into something like deep storage.

David Seamands explains what happens when memories are left repressed:

Such repressed and fixated memories can never be forgotten. . . . The harder we try to keep bad memories out of conscious recall, the more powerful they become. Since they are not allowed to enter the door of our minds directly, they come into our personalities . . . in disguised and destructive ways. These denied problems go underwater and later reappear as certain kinds of physical illnesses, unhappy marital situations, and recurring cycles of spiritual defeat. [13]

To some extent, the mind's ability to repress is a safety

hatch, protecting you from being forced to deal with events that are too overwhelming for you at the moment. But if you want to be released from their grip, you will have to let the Father's healing power into them.

Buried memories are not forgotten. They are on file in your subconscious mind. Because they are not recognized, they are able to wreak havoc in your emotions undetected. The memories are actually surfacing through your responses such as fear, anxiety, anger, worry, insecurity, jealousy, and the like. However, because you don't consciously recognize them, you're not aware of what they are doing.

Remember these memories need not be of monumentally traumatic events. They can be things that were just difficult for you to process at that point of your development.

Let me insert a clarification here. I approach this idea of buried memories with caution. I know that many innocent people have been hurt by others' claims of repressed memories. It is not only very easy to manipulate this phenomenon but also easy for others, even with the most sincere motives, to implant false memories.

Here's what I mean by that. If you imagine something in detail, your brain does not know the difference between something you have imagined and something you have remembered. So if a trusted person suggests memories to a person who is honestly seeking the truth, it's possible to imagine a scene and mistake it for a memory. This is why I have told you several times and will repeat again, do not strain to recall memories. Let them surface naturally under the Holy Spirit's guidance. As you pray, ask the Spirit to stand guard over your mind and let only the truth emerge. Trust His ability to do that.

I strongly considered not even talking about this aspect of healing, because there is so much room for misunderstanding and misuse. But I could not avoid it because of how many times I have seen a real breakthrough in healing as buried memories surface. Most of the time a person is not claiming to have never previously remembered the event but is saying instead that she has not thought about it or remembered it in many years.

So I want you to ask the Father to reveal to you any buried memories that color your perceptions and create reactions that are out of proportion to the present situation. Don't strain for them or work to remember. Simply stay open to the Spirit's healing work, and when old, painful memories assert themselves, recognize them as a step in your healing. Do not fear them. Let the Father walk you through them, giving them new meaning and releasing you from their power. He won't recreate the past, but He will redefine it. He will replace lies with truth. He will break the power the past has over you.

Brain surgeons know that if they touch a particular place in the brain, it will activate memories as if they were happening at the very moment. Even sounds and smells will come flooding back. You can be absolutely certain that if a brain surgeon can touch your brain and activate memory, the Creator of your brain can do so too. Let Him do the work. You are the patient, not the surgeon. Put yourself in His hands.

Sometimes these memories will surface in dreams. You may not dream the actual event, but you will dream an event that evokes the same emotions or impressions. When these dreams are God's healing process, the impression from the dream will stay with you strongly for some time—maybe even days. Let the Spirit lead you in examining what He is bringing to you. What emotion did you feel in the dream? Now relax in Him and see if a memory of an event in which you felt that very emotion surfaces. You may dream the same emotion for many nights before the event comes to your conscious memory.

One woman, over a few weeks' time, had two distinct dreams. In one she was running away from something chasing her and knew that safety was on the other side of a body of water. Most of the dream consisted of her trying to run through waist-deep water and the frustration that she could not seem to make progress. In the other dream, she was in a car and arriving at a party of some sort. She could hardly wait for the car to come to a stop so she could join the party. The rest of the dream consisted of her trying to get her seat belt unhooked.

The emotions from both of these dreams lingered. Although the dreams were different, she gradually identified the same emotion she often felt as a teenager when her very strict father restricted her freedom to pursue some of her interests. She identified several memories of incidents that had evoked those emotions. She remembered that she felt both angry with her father and guilty about her feelings. By remembering these things, the Lord was able to help her forgive her father and herself. She was able to see the incidents in a new light and identify the good that had come out of them.

Let me emphasize that in most cases, these buried memories are not seismic events. When they happened, they seemed hurtful or traumatic at the moment. Their power lies in how you felt them or interpreted them in that moment. Many times, when you go back to these memories as an adult, the Lord will help you reinterpret them and place them into their true context.

For example, a friend who was going through an extended time of prayer for healing struggled with anger toward her mother. At some point, she remembered a time when, as a little girl, she fell out of a tree. She clearly remembered her panic. Her mother rushed out and, seeing that her daughter was not hurt, began to scold her and even spanked her. My friend has a clear emotional memory of how hurt she was by her mother's response. Emotional memory is the strongest kind of memory. In remembering events, your brain will nearly always give precedence to emotion.

Now having recalled that event and identified many of her present feelings with the same emotion she felt then, she could go back to that memory as an adult. She could view it through the eyes of a mother, having raised three boys herself. She could understand how her mother's fear at seeing her daughter fall and her relief at finding her unharmed was expressed inadequately and came across as anger. She could have compassion on her mother. The door was open to more healing.

⌒—REFLECT

Do you have any painful memories that try to surface, but you push them down again each time because they cause too much discomfort?

Would you be willing to bring them into the light and look at them?

If you are willing, will you just place them into Jesus' hands and say to Him, "Do with this as You will. Use this in my life to accomplish Your will. Please release me from the hold of this memory."

⌒—PRAYER

Lord, I surrender to Your compassion. I surrender to Your healing. I surrender to Your wisdom. Because I fully trust Your love for me, I cast all my burdens on You. You can do all things, and Your plans for me will come to pass. Amen.

HEAR HIS HEART

*"Send forth your light and your truth,
let them guide me" (Ps. 43:3).*

UPROOT BITTERNESS

See to it that no one misses the grace of God and that no bitter root grows up to cause trouble and defile many (Heb. 12:15).

Your memories of childhood may be primarily happy. You may remember your parents as loving and supportive. But your parents were not perfect. The hurtful things they did or said that were stored in your memory and filed away for future use may not have been intentional. They may not even have been wrong. Their power lies only in how you perceived them at the moment. And, being human, no doubt your parents did or said things out of frustration or weariness or momentary anger that hurt you.

Before the age of eight or so, your universe was too narrow for you to be able to factor into an experience such things as the other person's emotional state or even another person's unique way of expressing himself or herself. So if a child's mother has a moment of impatience, the child cannot reason, "My mother is having a bad day." The child will interpret the situation as, "I'm bad. My mother doesn't like me." Your mind's filing system is filled with such impressions, and they are real to you. They live in your memory.

Maybe, on the other hand, your childhood memories are not pleasant. Maybe you remember your parents or the significant adults in your life as selfish or cruel. You will need to revisit some of those memories and the perceptions formed from an adult perspective. Your parents might have been doing the best they could, however inadequate or twisted that was. It will help you to remember that whatever they did came from their own wounded state. Anger expressed at you might have been anger they felt at themselves. Like you, for them every new event was linked to a series of files filled with lies. So they have passed on their filed memories and the accompanying emotions that will poison you too. In a way, you have inherited their old files.

Sandra D. Wilson makes these observations:

As children, we believed that the image of ourselves that we saw mirrored in our parents' faces and in their behaviors toward us accurately reflected our true identities. . . . Young children lack the reasoning skills to figure out that what they were in their parents' faces and hear in their voices reflects and echoes who the parent is, not who the child is. Children have no way of knowing that even the most loving parents are marred mirrors. . . . All parents are wounded to some degree by their own hurting and hurtful parents. As a result, parents may unintentionally send confusing and distressing messages to their children.[14]

As you pray, ask the Father to clean out those files. You may not need to consciously remember an event in order to surrender the emotion to the Father. Simply ask Him to "move over the

surface of the deep" of your memories, deleting files that are
skewing your current perceptions. As David Seamands explains,
"Often we are not able to pinpoint particular experiences or hap-
penings. Instead . . . it can be an aggregate of surrounding
influences, an all-pervasive atmosphere which encompasses us
with a whole set of generalized memories which require healing." [15]

There were experiences in childhood with others besides
your parents. Your siblings, your friends, your peers, and your
teachers all had great impact on you. You have memories that
probably caused some root of bitterness to take hold, and now
that bitterness grows fruit in your relationships.

Here's how those kinds of memories often surface. The
more emotion that is attached to an event, the more memory
cues you will associate with it. When a very hurtful episode
occurs that causes great anger, hurt, or resentment in you,
your brain will store it as episodic memory. Episodic memory
means that in storing the event in your memory, you have
memorized many physical details. You can recall the room, the
arrangement of the furniture, the stance and tone and facial
expression of the other person, sounds and smells that were
present, and other physical aspects. You can recreate the scene
in your mind with much detail. Because of this, you often
stumble across triggers that bring that memory out of storage.

Now the very nature of memory is that it is making the past
present. As Eugene Peterson says, "Memory . . . is vigorously
present tense, selecting out of the storehouse of the past,

retrieving and arranging images and insights, and then hammering them together for use in the present moment."[16] So at a moment's notice, a memory with strong emotional content can rush at you, and the anger or hurt can be as sharp as it was when the event first occurred. Most people have developed very good reflexes for pushing that memory down quickly, but the emotion it engaged cannot be so easily dismissed. The emotion sits just under the surface and will have to be expressed somewhere. It may be turned outward at others, or it may be turned inward against yourself.

Simply living in contact with other people affords many opportunities for being hurt or angered or disappointed. Your memory bank is filled with them. But another thing to understand about episodic memory is that you will remember it as it *seemed* to you. It is a subjective memory. For example, a person might remember her childhood home as very large, only to visit it as an adult and discover it is really quite small. In the same way, you have hurtful memories stored from your viewpoint. Many people have found that as they allow those memories to surface freely and look at them from an adult perspective, they can get a very different viewpoint.

I had a memory that used to surface often. I was very young. I can remember a particular piece of furniture, the certain way the light fell on my mother's face, the very way my parents were seated on the sofa, the stairway to my right. I told my parents something that was very important to me, and they laughed. I remember the absolute horror and shame I felt, because I thought I had said something that they thought was stupid and laughable.

Of course, now I know that I probably told my story in some cute childish way, and they were laughing because they thought it was cute. But that feeling or the fear of that feeling was a big part of my personality that I had to overcome. When I finally hit upon that memory and let it play all the way out and recognized that feeling as very familiar to me, I was able to identify the source of my fear of making mistakes and up-root the bitterness that memory had planted in me. Do you see that it's not what anyone else would identify as an important moment, but it was so important to me that my mind stored every detail about it? For a child with a personality different from mine, it may not have made any impact at all. My parents certainly did not intend harm to me in that incident.

So I encourage you to let those memories surface. Look at them from your adult perspective. Let the Holy Spirit over-write the old memory with the adult view. Little by little, you will find roots of bitterness being destroyed and new fruit growing in your life.

℮—REFLECT

Consider the words of Psalm 119:45: "I will walk about in freedom, for I have sought out your precepts." What is the Holy Spirit saying to you?

What memories is the Holy Spirit prompting that you need to let Jesus clean out, erasing the bitterness that has taken root?

ᴄ—PRAYER

I see now, Jesus, what You mean when You say, "If the Son sets you free, you will be free indeed" (John 8:36). I confess that my flesh is a tangled and chaotic web of lies and false impressions that are too complex and overwhelming for anyone but You to set right. Only You can set me free. Jesus, set me free. Amen.

HEAR HIS HEART

*Praise be to the LORD,
for he showed his wonderful love to me
when I was in a besieged city (Ps. 31:21).*

Scar Tissue

We take captive every thought to make it
obedient to Christ (2 Cor. 10:5).

The way our minds deal with the perceptions and memories of the past is to create defense mechanisms. "Because a lot of specifics are protected by our defense mechanisms and hidden in our buried memories, we cannot find emotional and spiritual relief from their onslaughts,"[17] this according to David Seamands. Defense mechanisms are behavior patterns that protect us from unpleasant feelings.

Some people lash out in anger out of proportion to the circumstance. Some make jokes about themselves or others. Some people criticize. Others blame those around them and refuse to take responsibility. Some people are overly defensive and sensitive to any perceived criticism. The list is endless.

Our minds have developed patterns of behavior that we exhibit automatically, without conscious thought. You might think of them as *flesh-patterns*. They are the ways your flesh— (the part of your inner self not fully surrendered to Christ's indwelling life; the places where you are still acting on your own power)—has learned to react to situations.

Defense mechanisms act like scar tissue, which develops over a wound to make it less sensitive. The defense mechanisms are not the main problem. It's the wound beneath them that needs healing. But the scar tissue has to be removed first so the wound can come to light. As long as we don't recognize our flesh-patterns, as long as we see our reactions as justified, we can continue to hide from the wound.

I have a dear friend whose flesh-pattern was to explode in anger at the tiniest offense (or imagined offense). Her ability to be utterly cruel and vicious was astounding, but she was always sorry later. As she began to experience deep emotional healing, she said to me, "I realized that the anger I spewed all over everyone around me is the hatred I feel for myself. I had to turn it outward to give myself some relief from the horrible feelings I carry around." Little by little, over a period of years, she began to lose her hostility toward herself, and her temper tantrums tapered off. Now she is free of them completely.

How did this work? First, she had to recognize the truth. Then she had to walk in the truth. At the start, she had more failures than victories. Yet each failure taught her something else about how her flesh-pattern was activated. When you are "walking out" a process of healing—consciously and deliberately choosing to walk in the light and the truth—even failures can become steps forward.

My friend continued to look to Jesus and away from herself, counting on His truth to overcome her lie. She began to take her thoughts to Him, making them His captives. Are you "convinced that he is able to guard what [you] have entrusted to him for that day" (2 Tim. 1:12)? My friend learned that Jesus is trustworthy and that He will honor your desire to surrender your thoughts to Him.

Ask the Holy Spirit to lead you into all truth on the matter of the flesh-patterns that act as scar tissue for you. Remember that you have had these patterns for most of your life and they seem instinctual to you. You don't think about them and decide to act in your flesh-pattern. Rather the action has overtaken you before you have time to think. This is about to change. The Holy Spirit will separate truth from lies for you as you allow Him to be your Teacher. His promise to you is this: "I will instruct you and teach you in the way you should go; I will counsel you and watch over you" (Ps. 32:8).

What is your flesh-pattern? What do you struggle with over and over again? What behaviors or attitudes do you use to protect yourself? Do you play the victim, mentally listing your offender's many faults and telling yourself how unfair and uncalled for such actions are? Or do you immediately accept all the blame and rehearse your own failings and feel that you deserve any hurt inflicted on you? Do you argue and defend yourself until you have had the final word? Do you take your anger out on someone else, watching for the next opportunity to explode? Do you eat, shop, or gossip?

Ask the Father to show you your flesh-patterns and what those defense mechanisms are protecting. Only when you recognize and define those patterns and stop using them to avoid the pain can you begin the discovery of the wound they are protecting.

℗—REFLECT

Write out Psalm 25:4-5, praying it phrase by phrase as you write it.

Keeping in mind that your flesh-patterns will be revealed completely to you over time, which ones do you immediately recognize? Write down what you are thinking. Ask the Spirit, by His laserlike power, to remove scar tissue so your wounds can be healed.

℗—PRAYER

Light of the World—Light that darkness cannot overcome—enlighten the eyes of my heart. Show me anything I need to see. I confess to You that my behaviors and ways of thinking are so familiar to me that it will be impossible for me to see them as they are unless You reveal them. Would You? I bring my thoughts into captivity to You. Amen.

HEAR HIS HEART

Praise the LORD, O my soul;
all my inmost being, praise his holy name.
Praise the LORD, O my soul,
and forget not all his benefits—
who forgives all your sins

and heals all your diseases,
who redeems your life from the pit
and crowns you with love and compassion,
who satisfies your desires with good things
so that your youth is renewed like the eagle's
(Ps. 103:1–5).

HEALING THE ROOT

They saw the fig tree withered from the roots. Peter remembered and said to Jesus, "Rabbi, look! The fig tree you cursed has withered!" (Mark 11:20–21).

Please don't think of this process of inner healing as mystical. I don't want to leave you with that impression. Don't imagine that it will require you to dredge up past hurts or scour your memory bank for offenses. Simply be aware of the probability that you have memories stored and cross-referenced in your subconscious that influence the way you think and respond to situations today. And remember that the healing power of the Father that flows through prayer is more than sufficient to strip those memories of their power over you.

As you let the Healer recreate the landscape of your subconscious mind, your job is simply to be still. You will become more aware of behaviors that once came instinctively and spontaneously. You will find yourself progressively more able to think about the behavior before acting it out.

Don't be discouraged if at first you only recognize a flesh-pattern when you are already finished with an episode. Recognizing it for what it is will be the first step to allowing God to dismantle it. Be patient with yourself. It is God who is at work in you to bring about the changes. Learn from Beth Moore's experience:

You may be wondering, "But what about the sins of our pasts?" Beloved, one of the times when Satan pounced on me most ferociously and used my past sins against me, I had already repented of those sins. They could no longer be used as sins against me. But here's the catch: They were still weaknesses! Why? Because I had asked God to forgive me, but I had never asked God to heal me completely, redeem my past, restore my life, sanctify me entirely, and help me forgive myself.[18]

God has already forgiven you. Now He is healing you. Put yourself in His hands. If you need to specifically and consciously remember an event, then the Spirit of God will bring it to your memory. If long-buried memories emerge, don't fear or resist them. Just be responsive to the powerful presence of Jesus with you, engaging memory only in order to heal.

When and if memories emerge, remember that the important thing is not what happened but how you *interpreted* what happened. As you remember, think about how it made you feel. What did it make you think? Can you connect that feeling from back then to feelings in the present? Let God begin to dismantle your flesh-patterns from their foundation. Let the tree wither from its roots.

Ask the Father to make you progressively new, old things passing away, new things coming.

ᴥ REFLECT

Pray slowly, reflectively and deliberately through Psalm 143:10:

> *Teach me to do your will,*
> *for you are my God;*
> *may your good Spirit*
> *lead me on level ground.*

Let an awareness of His presence settle on you and fill you. Let your mind see the reality of Him being fully with you. Let Him encourage you and speak to you about His love for you. Write out the things He impresses on your heart.

ᴥ PRAYER

Here I am, Lord. Speak. Your servant is listening. Amen.

HEAR HIS HEART

> *He does not treat us as our sins deserve*
> *or repay us according to our iniquities.*
> *For as high as the heavens are above the earth,*
> *so great is his love for those who fear him;*
> *as far as the east is from the west,*
> *so far has he removed our transgressions from us.*

As a father has compassion on his children,
so the LORD has compassion on those who fear him;
for he knows how we are formed,
he remembers that we are dust (Ps. 103:10–14).

9. Merriam-Webster's Collegiate Dictionary, 11th ed., see "wellspring."

10. H. Norman Wright, *Making Peace with Your Past* (Grand Rapids: Baker Book House, 1997), 41.

11. Marilee Sprenger, *Learning and Memory: The Brain in Action* (Alexandria, Va.: Association for Supervision and Curriculum Development, 1999), 37, 56.

12. Seamands, *Redeeming the Past,* 14–15.

13. Seamands, *Redeeming the Past,* 37.

14. Wilson, *Hurt People Hurt People*, 41.

15. Seamands, *Redeeming the Past,* 38.

16. Eugene H. Peterson, *Answering God* (San Francisco: HarperSanFrancisco, 1989), 117.

17. Seamands, *Redeeming the Past,* 70

18. Beth Moore, *When Godly People Do Ungodly Things* (Nashville: Broadman and Holman, 2002), 73.

SECTION THREE

Healing Your Relationships

HEALING FRUIT

"I am the vine; you are the branches. If a man remains in me and I in him, he will bear much fruit; apart from me you can do nothing" (John 15:5).

As you begin letting the healing power of the Father flow through your memories and your flesh-patterns, you'll discover that inner healing is being expressed in your relationships. When your inner healing starts to take hold, the way you relate to those around you will change. However, those people are used to the old you. They are conditioned to respond to you in a certain way, and it takes them some time to "relearn" you. Be patient.

Sometimes your inner healing can disrupt a relationship and throw it into crisis. Don't let that scare you. This probably means that the relationship has had underlying problems that have needed to be dealt with. For example, a friend of mine, through consistent prayer, experienced a powerful healing that allowed her not to feel unworthy of love. Before she had been very subservient and afraid ever to voice an opinion. She always felt intimidated, as though she had no right to her own thoughts.

When she began walking out her healing, she became less servile and compliant. Please understand, she didn't become aggressive or rebellious. She simply became a person. This was new to her husband and her children, and they had a hard time with it at first. She went through quite a time of testing, but God was so real to her and her healing had been so powerful that she eventually recreated her relationships with her family so that they were healthy. She learned that God is as able to heal her relationships as He is able to heal her memories.

The flesh-patterns in which you have operated are not new to you. They have been in place basically for all your life. Everyone who knows you, knows you to some extent by your flesh-patterns. Interestingly, the people closest to you often enable and engage your flesh-patterns. And your flesh-patterns encourage and activate their flesh-patterns in turn.

Why does this happen? Well, your family has formed your flesh-patterns, and you're usually drawn to those who keep engaging them because it's what you know. And even if it gets painful, you probably prefer the familiar to the unknown. Most of us do.

God, however, wants to set you free. He wants to dismantle your flesh-patterns from their foundation. For this to happen, the symptoms of your soul-wounds need to manifest themselves, driving you into God's arms. I wrote a book called *He Restores My Soul: A Forty-Day Journey Toward Personal Renewal*, which is about how to die to your flesh-patterns and receive the power of resurrection in their place. I explained it this way:

Does it seem to you that certain situations repeatedly bring out the same reactions in you? Do you often find yourself repeating destructive behavior patterns? Do you find that numerous situations arouse in you familiar emotions like anger, fear, envy, or shame?

When we react in the flesh, it is the tendency of our human nature to blame circumstances or to blame people around us. You may be able to pinpoint an outside cause, but that outside cause is not the ultimate source. God is always in the process of breaking the patterns established by your flesh. He allows you to be confronted with the same weaknesses over and over again. See these incidents for what they are: crucifixion moments.

At a crucifixion moment you are offered two choices: to react in the old way of your human nature or to react in the new way of the Spirit. When you choose to place blame on others, or feel martyred by circumstances beyond your control, you resuscitate your self-life. When, on the other hand, you choose to look away from the outside cause and accept the crucifying work of the Spirit, you begin, little by little, to let the old nature die and the new nature emerge. [19]

It's not unusual to find, for example, an overly sensitive woman married to an overly critical man. Or a person who resents authority continually finding herself under the authority of an overly controlling person. Do you see why the very arrangement of your circumstances and relationships, even those that seem to add to your problems, is the context in which healing will occur?

Your healing also has the potential to trigger healing in those around you. When your flesh-patterns are replaced by new Spirit-created responses, the Spirit flowing through you can touch a chord in others. It is He, not you, reaching out to those around you. His touch has power in it—power to draw, power to transform, power to bring truth.

⁓ REFLECT

Do you see that those whom God has placed around you often activate your flesh-patterns? List specifics as you now see them.

Thank God specifically for every person and every circumstance that forces your flesh-patterns into the open. Release any past efforts to force people or circumstances into a form that would not challenge your flesh-patterns.

⁓ PRAYER

Holy Spirit, let me be the vessel that contains Your life. Let Your healing flow through me. Teach me how to be the branch that abides in You, bearing Your fruit. Amen.

HEAR HIS HEART

"Let your light shine before men, that they may see your good deeds and praise your Father in heaven"
(Matt. 5:16).

INVITATION TO WHOLENESS
"Forgive us our debts, as we also have forgiven our debtors"
(Matt. 6:12).

Healing is a lifelong process of growing into wholeness. It is not a one-time event. As you learn the ways of the Healer and the power of His healing, you enter into a cooperative interaction with Him. He is always healing. You are always receiving His healing. A healing of one flesh-pattern and its source opens the way for another healing. An uninterrupted undercurrent of prayer is operative in you all the time. This is the reality of Christ in you.

Central to the healing journey is forgiveness: forgiving those who have wronged you and receiving forgiveness for the offenses you have committed. Forgiving others is one of the most freeing, most healing, actions you will ever take. But let's save that for another day. First, before you can forgive others, you must acknowledge your own sins, admit your own guilt.

Not only do buried memories of hurt quietly poison your life, so does unconfessed sin. David put it this way: "My guilt has overwhelmed me like a burden too heavy to bear" (Ps. 38:4). In coming to a place of acknowledging your own sin, you will be more able to forgive others.

As you pray, let the Spirit bring to the surface the attitudes and behaviors you have been justifying and rationalizing. Will you right now name them "sins"? As you let the Spirit spotlight sins, remember that you have likely assigned to each sin an outside cause—something that justifies the sin in your mind. The outside cause may indeed be wrong, but it does not have to cause you to sin. Today you must not coddle that sin inside you. Face the truth and name it. Quit assigning blame elsewhere. As Solomon observed, "The wisdom of the prudent is to give thought to their ways, but the folly of fools is deception" (Prov. 14:8).

So let the Spirit do the searching. As He brings a thought to mind, surrender to Him. He is not chastising you. He is offering you wholeness and healing. Admit to yourself that you have hurt others, just as others have hurt you. When appropriate, go to the person you have hurt and ask for his or her forgiveness.

You have now recognized that you have hurts and wounds that were inflicted on you by others, even if unintentionally. The people who hurt you were probably acting out of their own woundedness and the lies they believe about themselves and others. It's possible that they don't even know they've hurt you. Doesn't it make sense that, in some cases, you are the one hurting someone else for the same reasons?

Now this is not the time to beat up on yourself. That's not my goal in teaching this at all. The purpose is to bring everything out into the light and leave nothing hidden in the darkness. When you boldly recognize that you have caused pain to others, you will be much more willing to forgive those who have caused you pain. You will begin to have compassion on them, as the Lord has compassion on you (see Eph. 4:32).

I want you to fully receive into your experience the forgiveness that has always been yours. God did not wait for you to make the first move—He took the initiative to bridge the gap that sin created. He forgave you at the Cross. He "forgave it forward." But hanging on to a sin and covering it over and making room for it keeps you from the full experience of His forgiveness. It keeps you bound to and operating according to a lie. So please repent—change the direction of your thoughts. Reorient your mind to the truth.

⌒—REFLECT

Consider Psalm 119:32: "I run in the path of your commands, for you have set my heart free." Write out what these words are saying to you right now.

Let the Spirit bring to mind those sins of which He is convicting you. He is not scolding you or condemning you. He is setting you free. Let His conviction of sin be a reminder of His love for you. He is not willing to see your life compromised by sin. Read these words from Hebrews 12:5-11:

"My son, do not make light of the Lord's discipline, and do not lose heart when he rebukes you,

because the Lord disciplines those he loves,
and he punishes everyone he accepts as a son."

Endure hardship as discipline; God is treating you as sons. For what son is not disciplined by his father? If you are not disciplined (and everyone undergoes discipline), then you are illegitimate children and not true sons. Moreover, we have all had human fathers who disciplined us and we respected them for it. How much more should we submit to the Father of our spirits and live! Our fathers disciplined us for a little while as they thought best; but God disciplines us for our good, that we may share in his holiness. No discipline seems pleasant at the time, but painful. Later on, however, it produces a harvest of righteousness and peace for those who have been trained by it.

Write down the things He is impressing on you.

PRAYER

Lord, I surrender to Your love, calling me to break my ties with sin. Because I so completely trust Your love for me, Your grace toward me, and Your plan for me, I choose to face my own sins and let Your healing forgiveness flow through me, in me, to me. I receive Your love. Amen.

HEAR HIS HEART

Keep your servant also from willful sins;
may they not rule over me.
Then will I be blameless,
innocent of great transgression.
May the words of my mouth
and the meditation of my heart
be pleasing in your sight,
O LORD, my Rock and my Redeemer
(Ps. 19:13–14).

YOUR FREEDOM

But where sin increased, grace increased all the more
(Rom. 5:20).

God is not convicting you of sin to condemn you but to free you. He is not surprised at your sin—He has already made a way for that sin to be separated from you and stricken from your record. He wants you to experience the forgiveness He has for you, and that requires your acknowledgment and repentance.

It's very likely that as your memories are being cleansed and healed, you will discover the sins those inner wounds have given birth to. You must honestly acknowledge that the sins you have committed have been harmful to others, just as the sins others have committed against you have brought you harm. The very same spiritual and emotional dynamics that caused you to sin against others are what have caused others to sin against you.

This realization will allow you to replace condemnation and anger with grace. The greater the offender's sin, the greater spiritual and emotional void and toxicity it reveals. Let the bitterness be replaced with compassion. Would you allow the Spirit to make you able to forgive others as God, in Christ, forgave you? (Eph. 4:32).

The processes in your brain that create memory are fascinating. Your brain divides its work into highly specialized functions. One area analyzes and files smell, another area handles visual input, yet another deals with auditory input, and so on. One area deals with factual information and another with emotion. Even within these specialized areas, the breakdown is even more detailed. For example, in the occipital lobe, where visual information is translated, labeled, and filed, a certain area deals with color, another with shape, still another with movement. Then there's size and depth. And the list goes on.

When your brain encodes a memory, neurons from all these different areas create a bond, a pathway, called an *engram*. The physical structure of your brain actually changes and is different than it was before you stored that memory. Therefore, some cue that activates one aspect of a given memory will then automatically activate the whole engram. I just find that fascinating.

The more you relive a given engram, dwelling on it and focusing on all the emotions, the stronger the neural connections—the memory pathways—become. As you surrender to the Healer's work, He will help you find the balance between remembering for the purpose of healing and reliving painful, hurtful memories for the purpose of keeping them alive.

You can deal with a painful memory one of two ways. You can let your flesh be master. In that case, the memory will activate anger and resentment. You can feel the anger as if the incident had just happened. As you rehearse the memory, you actually strengthen the emotions connected to it. You get angrier every time you go over it again. When you relive the incident in depth, the details become more fixed in your factual memory, which also brings into play your emotional memory. You can keep the incident alive until the end of your life if you so choose. If you choose this path, remembering an incident that had been buried will be destructive rather than healing.

A woman came to me asking for long-term prayer for emotional healing. She had debilitating anger at her family, including her ex-husband and her children. She, however, did not call it anger. She insisted she had forgiven them. Yet she actually brought with her a journal detailing every painful memory she could dredge up. Her agenda was to have me listen to her read her journal and then join her in her self-pitying outrage.

When, instead, I challenged her to rethink these painful memories from another perspective, she was offended and certain that I could not understand all the pain that had been inflicted upon her. She could not find relief from her pain because she chose to remember in order to feed her anger rather than to let her anger go.

In contrast, the second way to deal with painful memories is to let the Spirit have control. You can allow Him to lead you into the truth. You can give Him your heart so He can shape and mold it to conform to Jesus' prayer: "Father, forgive them, for they do not know what they are doing" (Luke 23:34). The person or persons who hurt you may not have known how much harm they were doing. They were probably acting from their own misguided, sin-clouded wounds and needs, thinking of the moment, not of future ramifications. In many situations, the people who hurt you had no idea how you would interpret their words or actions.

Can you let it go? It may take you time to do so, and you will need the Spirit's help. But it really will set you free.

Let me suggest something, based on the understanding of how memories are stored in your brain as engrams. Do you see that it is actually a physical arrangement of the components of your brain, which is a physical organ? What if, after having dealt in healing ways with the memory, we just ask the Creator to dismantle and weaken those neural connections that make up the storage place of that memory? He won't change the past, and the ramifications of the event remembered are intricately woven throughout your personality. But why could He not simply weaken an engram's connections and render it powerless? I think that sometimes He might do just that.

᧔—REFLECT

Are there any hurtful memories that you have been rehearsing and keeping on life support? Will you let them go now? Write down a word or phrase that will name the memory for you, and let the act of writing it down be your act of surrender.

∂—PRAYER

Spirit of Truth, show me the truth about those whom I need to forgive. Pour Your love for them into my heart. I release them to You. I choose Your freedom over the tyranny of anger and bitterness. I will forgive others as fully and freely as You have forgiven me. Amen.

HEAR HIS HEART

If you, O LORD, kept a record of sins,
O Lord, who could stand?
But with you there is forgiveness;
therefore you are feared (Ps. 130:3–4).

LEAVE THE PAST BEHIND

"If the Son sets you free, you will be free indeed
(John 8:36).

Your own confession and repentance is working hand-in-hand with your progress in forgiving others. You are entering into the freedom of letting go of bitterness.

Think of anger and bitterness as tethers that keep you tied to a past event. As long as you hold on to the resentment, you are a prisoner to the wrong done you. It keeps pulling you back, making you live in the past. As you forgive your offender, imagine Jesus cutting those tethers. With your mind's eye, look closely at the severed ends now hanging loose from your waist. Affirm the truth—say it out loud: "I am no longer a prisoner to (name the offense). Jesus Himself has broken its hold over me. I'm leaving the past behind and moving forward to what lies ahead."

Don't be discouraged if some of the old anger or the old flesh-patterns still surface. Corrie ten Boom had a wonderful explanation for this in her book *Tramp for the Lord*. She referred to it as "the ding-dong effect." Satan no longer has hold of the bell's rope. He is no longer ringing the bell, but there are a few last ding-dongs as the bell gradually becomes still.

Forgiving is usually a process. Even when a person seems to be able to completely forgive in a single act, that act is likely to be the culmination of a process. Once you have entered into the process of forgiving your offender, you begin to become free. That freedom will gradually manifest itself in your life and experience if you continue in the process no matter what directions your emotions take at any given moment.

When the old anger asserts itself in your emotions, tell yourself the truth. "I have forgiven (name your offender). This anger and bitterness no longer has the power to tie me to the past. These emotions are not my truth. I choose to die to this flesh-based anger and live in the power of the resurrection. The life of Jesus flowing through me is cleansing me of all anger. I refuse the anger. I embrace the life of Christ in me."

Marsha's parents had been neglectful and irresponsible. Marsha and her brothers and sisters were taken from their parents time and again to be placed in a variety of foster homes, none of which was a positive experience. As an adult, the anger and resentment Marsha had toward her parents had taken its toll. Her feelings were so intense that she had to develop a range of defense mechanisms to protect herself and keep her memories at bay.

Through prolonged prayer for inner healing, she came to terms with the fact that her parents were deeply wounded people who did the best they were capable of doing. Gradually, the Holy Spirit dismantled her anger from the ground up, withered it from the root. Marsha was able to forgive her parents, free herself from the past to which she had been bound, and progressively learn new ways of living. It was a painful, difficult process, but not nearly as painful and difficult as remaining a slave to her bitterness. Even now, she sometimes has a flash of the old anger. But she does not accept it as her truth. Forgiveness is an act of her will, empowered and carried to fruition by the Spirit of God.

ᴏ—REFLECT

What tethers to the past have been broken? Write them down. Celebrate your freedom.

ᴏ—PRAYER

Jesus, when You make me free, then I will be free indeed. I want to be free. I refuse to be bound to the past. I am letting go of what lies behind and reaching out for what lies ahead. I am taking hold of that for which You took hold of me. Amen.

HEAR HIS HEART

"Forgetting what is behind and straining toward what is ahead, I press on toward the goal to win the prize for which God has called me heavenward in Christ Jesus" (Phil. 3:13–14).

COME INTO THE LIGHT

*"But whoever lives by the truth comes into the light,
so that it may be seen plainly that what he has
done has been done through God" (John 3:21).*

As you become more sure-footed in negotiating the territory of healing and wholeness, as you learn to live in the prayer interaction always going on between you and Christ dwelling within you, your desire for healing at every level will grow deeper. You won't be satisfied with relationships that are not whole. Your confidence in the power of God for every need will give you the courage to begin praying for the healing of a broken or damaged relationship.

This healing for which you long involves the will and mind-set of another person—a person over whom you have no control. How can you confidently expect healing in a relationship if the other person involved is not responsive? You are about to learn one of the most wonderful prayer secrets!

The power of God that flows into situations through prayer has no limitations. None. As you pray with tenacious faith, faith that is stouthearted and doesn't fold in the heat of battle, the very same God who knows exactly how to get your attention also knows how to get the attention of the person for whom you are praying. You can surrender all control to the One who knows the secrets of every person's heart and who knows how to break through any barrier and tear down any stronghold.

So pray for God to move in the innermost being of that person to bring wholeness and teach truth that will eventually work itself out in a healed relationship. Just as God reached out to you, moving you to seek healing, so He will reach out to those for whom you pray. Be as patient with that person as God has been with you.

ᏩᎧ—REFLECT

Name the relationships that you are surrendering to God for His healing power.

ᏩᎧ—PRAYER

Lord, I lay this relationship on Your altar. It is Yours. Do in it and through it what You desire. I will be a living offering to You. Use me however You want to initiate healing in this relationship. I relinquish all my machinations, all my anxiety, all my manipulations. You do all the work. I focus my energies on seeking Your kingdom and Your righteousness. Amen.

HEAR HIS HEART

"But seek first his kingdom and his righteousness, and all these things will be given to you as well.

Therefore do not worry about tomorrow, for tomorrow will worry about itself. Each day has enough trouble of its own" (Matt. 6:33–34).

WATER IN THE WILDERNESS

*Water will gush forth in the wilderness
and streams in the desert.
The burning sand will become a pool,
the thirsty ground bubbling springs.
In the haunts where jackals once lay,
grass and reeds and papyrus will grow (Isa. 35:6–7).*

Do you fear that there is no hope? Do you feel that this relationship is ruined and there is no way to reconstruct it? Then it's time for you to think about the One to whom you are bringing this wasteland.

He makes dry bones live again (Ezek. 37:1–14). He causes streams to flow in the desert (Isa. 35:6). He makes a root to grow out of dry ground (53:2). He turns a mountain into a way (40:4). He makes water gush from a rock (Exod. 17:5–6). He causes a dead and barren womb to give birth to a nation (Gen. 21:1–7). Because of Him, a crucifixion becomes a prelude to a resurrection. Bringing life out of death is His way.

Do you bring Him a relationship that is barren desert land? That is prime ground for the healing power of Jehovah Rapha. Wrap it in prayer. "What Your will is in heaven for this relationship, let it be so on earth. Let Your kingdom come in this relationship."

Prayer is birthing the will of God out of the spiritual realm and onto the earth. As you look at this situation and it seems overwhelming to you, spiritually take the birthing position. Recognize that labor pains are part of the process, and every labor pain is bringing the end that much closer. As you move into the final stages of the process, the labor pains increase both in intensity and duration. Do not be discouraged.

You are like Paul, who told the Galatians, "My dear children, for whom I am again in the pains of childbirth until Christ is formed in you" (Gal. 4:19). Paul was specifically talking about his praying for others to be conformed to Christ. We, too, are involved with God through prayer in the final outcome.

There is no guarantee that when the relationship is made whole it will be as you expected it to be. But it will be right, and you will be satisfied. So let God do His work in His way. Keep your focus on Him, not on your expectations. My son Brantley wrote this prayer: "God, knowing You is my concern. Everything else is Your concern." Make that your prayer as well.

In this relationship, you are acting and responding from a different motivation than before. You don't have to protect your wounded places anymore. You are a new person. Gradually, the other person will change in response to you. It won't be immediate. And it may not be the change you envisioned. But don't get discouraged. Just be the new you, letting Jesus flow through you in every situation. Jesus will know how to handle it.

As you look back, do you see that Jesus was always wooing you? That He was always whispering a promise of healing to you? Even at your most discouraged, something in you kept seeking wholeness. Remember? It is the same with the person for whom you are praying. The very same Jesus is working in that person's heart and life. Let Jesus do what only Jesus can do.

⌒—REFLECT

Write out your personal statement of surrender.

PRAYER

Lord, I know You are able to accomplish anything that concerns me. In Your sovereignty, You knew that this relationship and this situation would be in my life right now. You have a plan in place for how to bring healing, and I trust Your plans for me. Out of this death, You will bring life. I believe. Amen.

HEAR HIS HEART

"I am the resurrection and the life" (John 11:25).

19. Jennifer Kennedy Dean, *He Restores My Soul: A Forty-Day Journey Toward Personal Renewal* (Nashville: Broadman and Holman, 1999), 32–33.

Living in Wholeness

PROGRESSING IN WHOLENESS

The path of the righteous is like the first gleam of dawn,
shining ever brighter till the full light of day (Prov. 4:18).

The journey toward wholeness continues your whole life long; the path, like the light of dawn, growing clearer and brighter with each step. The more healing you experience, the more you will recognize your further need for healing. As you discover for yourself the power of God to heal, the process will become less intimidating and overwhelming. You know that if you rest in God, He will bring everything into focus. So even though this healing will be a lifetime journey, don't think of it as a lifetime struggle.

As your healing progresses, you will also become more aware of the reality of the spiritual realm. You will learn that all of life has a spiritual dimension, and that spiritual aspect is the driving force and purpose. Paul says, "Set your minds on things above, not on earthly things" (Col. 3:2). Elsewhere he tells us to "fix our eyes not on what is seen, but on what is unseen. For what is seen is temporary, but what is unseen is eternal" (2 Cor. 4:18). In other words, the invisible aspects of a situation are not fleeting or momentary, but the visible aspects are. Wherever you are, look for the kingdom.

Susan had an unreasonable boss. He piled more work on her than she could possibly do within the deadlines he imposed. That's what she could see, and as she focused there she became stressed and angry. One day she decided to take her eyes off the situation as it looked from earth and put her eyes on the kingdom. What flesh-pattern was coming to the surface because of her situation? She began to ask the Lord to show her what He was doing and why He had her in this stressful situation.

She soon realized that she feared addressing the situation with her boss because she thought he would fire her. That led her to understand that her faith was misplaced—she was trusting her boss's power over her rather than God's power for her. When she addressed the situation with her boss, he was amazed to find out that he was being unreasonable. Because she never said anything about it, he assumed she was just fine with the way things were. When Susan began to look for the kingdom, recognizing the spiritual dynamics of her situation, God was able to use it to further mature her and move her toward wholeness.

As you recognize the spiritual dynamics of each situation that comes into your life, train yourself to focus on growing through it. What emotions and responses are brought to the surface by a situation? Could it be that your responses are revealing hidden toxins, and the Healer is drawing them out in order to rid you of them? God could be allowing certain circumstances in your life to further your healing. They can act as a spiritual poultice, drawing out infection.

ᴥ REFLECT

What situation right now is God using as a spiritual poultice?

Will you ask Him to help you replace any anxiety or anger you have in this situation with thanksgiving for the further healing God wants to use it for? Focus on each word of this verse:

"Do not be anxious about anything, but in everything, by prayer and petition, with thanksgiving, present your requests to God. And the peace of God, which transcends all understanding, will guard your hearts and your minds in Christ Jesus"
(Phil. 4:6–7).

ᴥ PRAYER

Thank You, Lord, for every situation that is bringing out the flesh-patterns in me. I acknowledge that this is part of the healing I have asked You for. You are answering my heart's cry for wholeness. I place myself in Your healing hands and gratefully walk the path You have laid out. Amen.

HEAR HIS HEART

"Consider it pure joy, my brothers, whenever you face trials of many kinds, because you know that the testing of your faith develops perseverance. Perseverance

must finish its work so that you may be mature and complete, not lacking anything" (James 1:2–4).

The Finishing Touch

Do not conform any longer to the pattern of this world,
but be transformed by the renewing of your mind. Then
you will be able to test and approve what God's will is
—his good, pleasing and perfect will (Rom. 12:2).

As you learn to live in wholeness, you'll become more and more familiar with the reality of having to let go. Another word for that is *relinquishment.* It means "leave behind; give up; release; to give over possession or control of." [20] When you find the secret of relinquishment, you have come upon one of the most powerful weapons in the healing arsenal. I call this a weapon because many people mistakenly think of it as a weak or passive word. In its spiritual context, it is an aggressive and strong word.

The ability to relinquish is rooted in a full and total confidence in God. Your ability to relinquish grows with your experience of God's faithfulness. When you have relied on Him and seen how trustworthy He is, you'll find that relinquishing your control comes more easily. "Your promises have been thoroughly tested, and your servant loves them" (Ps. 119:140). At first, relinquishment will be difficult and feel risky, but with practice it will become your way of living. You will feel at home in it.

God has placed in your mind a hope and an expectation of healing and wholeness. This comes from Him. If "the whole creation has been groaning" to be renewed and restored, how much more have we who have been made in God's image (Rom. 8:22–23)! The Lord Himself has awakened this yearning in you. It is the vision He has given you, so hold on to it. But beware of the flesh-based tendency to decide that it is your job to bring the vision into being. It's God's vision—relinquish! Leave it to Him.

What is it you need, right now, to relinquish? A relationship? A person's behavior? A circumstance in your life? A need or desire? A past hurt or disappointment? Here is the central question: Do you believe that God is fully able to manage every detail of any situation? Do you believe that He has a plan that He will work out in His own way and in His own time? Do you believe that God's will is "good, pleasing, and perfect" (Rom. 12:2)? Then let healing flow through relinquishment.

Haley loved her teenage daughter and wanted only the best for her. And Haley knew what was best. She was sure of it. If her daughter would lose weight, Haley thought, then she would be happier with herself. If she were happier with herself, she would be more motivated in school. If she were more motivated in school, she would make better grades, get into a better college, have a better career, make more money, find a wonderful husband, and have perfect children.

You see where this is going. It all hinged on her daughter losing weight. This was the focus of Haley's existence—or so it seemed to her friends. She did everything she could think of and made her daughter's life miserable. In desperation, she came to me and said, "Would you pray with me that my daughter will lose weight?" So began Haley's journey toward learning the power of relinquishment.

As we talked, she identified one of her motivations for wanting her daughter to lose weight. Secretly, she feared that it reflected badly on her. She was embarrassed that her daughter was so heavy. She needed to relinquish her flesh-pattern of worrying about what others would think of her. So each time she began to feel angry or stressed about her daughter's weight, she confessed her pride and chose to die to it. She embraced the opportunity to have her flesh-pattern brought out into the open where she could recognize it and turn away from it.

She found that she also wanted her daughter to lose weight because she wanted her to be happy and to feel confident. I asked her if she believed that God wanted her daughter to be happy. She agreed that He did. I asked her if God knew exactly what would bring her daughter happiness. We agreed that a trusting walk with Him would be the key to her daughter's happiness, not her weight. And that's what we began to pray for her daughter. The tension in their house gradually dissipated, and the relationship improved. Haley quit trying to control her daughter's eating habits. Her daughter has not lost weight, but she is involved in a small group Bible study and is growing spiritually. Her countenance, once dour, has become cheerful and happy. It is only the beginning.

Haley has been freed of a burden. She felt that it was up to her to make her daughter happy. Now she knows that it is God's work in her daughter that will bring happiness, and Haley can just enjoy the relationship. She has learned that when she allows her thoughts to be transformed and brought into alignment with God's, she finds His will to be good, pleasing, and perfect.

REFLECT

Where do you need to relinquish control in your relationships in order to see healing flow? As you write down what comes to mind, make your writing an act of relinquishment in itself.

PRAYER

Sovereign Father, I will let You be fully in control. I will not try to impose my will or my expectations on those around me or on my relationships. You are the Potter, I am the clay. You are the Shepherd, I am a sheep of Your pasture. I am Yours. Amen.

HEAR HIS HEART

"Peter turned and saw that the disciple whom Jesus loved was following them. . . . When Peter saw him,

he asked, "Lord, what about him?" Jesus answered, "If I want him to remain alive until I return, what is that to you? You must follow me" (John 21:20–22).

A LIVING OFFERING

Therefore, I urge you, brothers, in view of God's mercy, to offer your bodies as living sacrifices, holy and pleasing to God—this is your spiritual act of worship (Rom. 12:1).

How does full relinquishment express itself? Like everything else in this journey, as you learn its power, it becomes more than something you do only at certain times. It becomes a way of life—a living surrender, a living sacrifice.

My son Brantley recently taught this about surrender: "Let your every prayer become, 'God, all I want is what You want. Whatever You want to do, let it flow through me.'" Do you realize that when God flows through you, His healing power is flowing? Because He Himself is our healing—not just our Healer, but our healing.

Christ in you begins to flow through you like rivers of living water. Wherever a river flows, it changes the landscape. Nothing in the river's path remains the same. In the same way, Jesus rearranges the landscape of your mind, your will, and your emotions. They become the reflection of Him. They become the conduits through which He expresses Himself. Like Him, you will learn to say, "I have come . . . not to do my will but to do the will of him who sent me" (John 6:38). Over the course of your life, your will and your desires are being shaped to match His. He is using everything in your life to shape you into what He has destined you for (Rom. 8:29).

His healing power flows through you and from you. As you lay aside your old patterns of behavior and ways of thinking, your growing wholeness will impact those around you. Why? Because you are navigating new territory, walking a new path. When the Israelites crossed over the Jordan River into the land of Canaan, they were told to keep their eyes on the ark of the covenant, the symbol of God's presence. You, too, must keep your eyes on the Lord, and "then you will know which way to go, since you have never been this way before" (Josh. 3:4). What an adventure you embarked on!

I want to encourage you to walk in the wholeness and healing that unfolds more every day. The old ways don't work anymore. Learn the new ways.

As you walk with the Healer, you will have a different perspective on all situations. Every situation that God allows in your life has the potential to bring deeper healing and greater growth and maturity. When you respond to situations from this perspective, the whole texture of your life changes. Events, circumstances, and personalities will not define your days. You will be defining your life more purposefully, based on your values and beliefs. You'll be impacted by your reactions, of course, but you won't be a slave to them anymore. This is our freedom in Christ.

A friend of mine wrote this to me: "It used to be that when anyone around me was in a bad mood, I immediately thought it was directed at me. So I became angry and defensive. If someone else was in a bad mood, then I was forced to be in a bad mood. But I'm a new woman now. I'll decide my own mood, thank you!"

If the Son makes you free, you are free indeed.

ᕁ—REFLECT

How can relinquishment make more room for healing in your life?

ᕁ—PRAYER

Father, all I want is what You want. Amen.

HEAR HIS HEART

"It is for freedom that Christ has set us free. Stand firm, then, and do not let yourselves be burdened again by a yoke of slavery" (Gal. 5:1).

GOD'S WORKMANSHIP

But I trust in you, O LORD;
I say, "You are my God."
My times are in your hands (Ps. 31:14–15).

You are a person of destiny. Before you were born, God
had assigned you a purpose—a reason for being. You do not
exist by chance. Nothing about you is random. He has been
bringing you into that destiny from the moment of your con-
ception—in fact, even before that. In the circumstances that
led up to your birth, in the generations of your ancestors, and
that which was passed from one generation to the next, in the
time assigned you in history—all were laying the foundation
for your destiny.

The process of healing is part of your progress toward
your destiny. Your wounds have set the stage for God to move
in your life and form you into "that for which Christ Jesus
took hold of" you (Phil. 3:12). What has been formed in you
on your journey from woundedness to wholeness has made
your life richer than it would have been if you had never been
wounded. I know that may be hard to accept, but I believe
with all my heart that it's true. The beautifully designed, intricately woven, brilliantly created masterpiece that you are
becoming owes its depth and beauty to the method of the Master who is forming you. Your wounds can become beautiful in
His hands. Just think of Jesus' wounds.

The body of His resurrection was perfect and eternal. It is the very body in which He ascended from earth to take His place at the right hand of the Father. This perfect, resurrected body retained its scars.

How often our pride, or our mistaken sense that we need to present a perfect front to those in our care, causes us to think of our wounds and our scars as something to hide; something ugly; something demeaning; something that lessens our value. But look at Jesus. Look at what Jesus thought of His wounds. "Here, Thomas. Look at My wounds. Touch My scars. These are the proof of My resurrection. I bear the marks of death, but I am alive!" Jesus knew His wounds were beautiful.

Thomas said, "Unless I see the nail marks in his hands and put my finger where the nails were, and put my hand into his side, I will not believe it" (John 20:25). My friend, hurting people are doubting the life of Christ in us, you and me. "Unless I see your wounds, I will not believe it. Unless I see your scars I cannot trust your message of hope and resurrection."

. . . At the places where I am broken, the power of Christ is authenticated in me for others. Where I have submitted to the crucifixion, the resurrection is put on display. I can say, "Look at my wounds. Touch my scars. I have death-wounds, but I am alive." I can wear my wounds without shame. They tell a resurrection story.[21]

Do you feel angry with God about your wounds? You can admit that anger to Him. He already knows about it. Express all of it to Him, and you will find His healing flowing even more. Move to a moment when you can, even without feeling it, thank Him for what He is creating out of the chaos and the hurts in your life. Praise does not change your circumstances, but it alters your viewpoint.

Who are you that you would not have been unless you had experienced the hurts in your life? What do you know that you could not have known apart from the disappointments you have suffered? What can you do that you learned in the crucible of your pain?

◇—REFLECT

Can you see how your scars are the very instruments of healing for those around you? Spend some time thinking about and describing the beauty of your wounds.

◇—PRAYER

My Lord, thank You for accepting my feelings as they are. Thank You for loving me enough to let me express myself honestly to You. My heart is safe when it rests in You. Amen.

HEAR HIS HEART

But we have this treasure in jars of clay to show that this all-surpassing power is from God and not from us. We are hard pressed on every side, but not crushed; perplexed, but not in despair; persecuted, but not abandoned; struck down, but not destroyed. We always carry around in our body the death of Jesus, so that the life of Jesus may also be revealed in our body (2 Cor. 4:7–10).

THE SURGEON'S SCALPEL

Before a word is on my tongue
you know it completely, O LORD (Ps. 139:4).

As you deal with your emotions and your memories, be completely honest with God. You don't need to have acceptable feelings or use cautious words. You won't shock the Almighty. Before a word is even on your tongue, He knows all about it. Before a thought has taken the shape of words, while it is still unformed and raw, He knows it completely.

Look at Simon Peter's experience.

"Simon, Simon, Satan has asked to sift you as wheat. But I have prayed for you, Simon, that your faith may not fail. And when you have turned back, strengthen your brothers" (Luke 22:31–32).

Jesus is telling Simon that Satan himself has asked permission to put him to the test. Obviously if Satan asked permission, God could have denied him that permission. No doubt, God had denied him numerous times before. But this time Satan was given permission to tempt Simon.

Why? God knew before the event that Peter would be defeated by the test. However, the Father also knew that he would repent and turn back again. So the Lord's plan was to use Peter's failure and subsequent repentance and restoration to strengthen believers. Peter's failure and Jesus' response to him would mark Peter for the rest of his life. But through Simon Peter's failure, God would be able to accomplish and teach things that He could not have if Peter had never fallen.

Have you ever thought of your failures in this light? It changes your point of view, doesn't it? I'm not saying that God is pleased when we fail, but I am saying that we don't need to give in to despair over it. We shouldn't give up, because God doesn't give up on us. As the psalmist wrote,

> As far as the east is from the west,
> so far has he removed our transgressions from us.
> As a father has compassion on his children,
> so the LORD has compassion on those who fear him;
> for he knows how we are formed,
> he remembers that we are dust (Ps. 103:12–14).

Deep down, when you've failed or been hurt by others' failings, you may have had the same feeling as Gideon: "'If the Lord is with us, why has all this happened to us?'" (Judg. 6:13). When a thought like this has begun to worm its way into your consciousness, have you pushed it back down? Did you think it was sinful or disrespectful? Did you fear that God would be angry with you? Take courage; He knows we are fragile, and He has compassion on us. Speak your true and honest feelings to Him. Do you feel angry with Him? Trust

His love enough to tell Him all about your feelings just as they are.

Think of it as surgery. You are opening yourself, exposing all the hidden hurt and anger. You've kept it hidden because it seemed wrong to you to let yourself be angry with God. But now you are laying your inner self open and letting Him reach in and pull all the anger out. It may hurt while it is happening, and you may be sore for a while afterward, but this is a healing wound.

∽—REFLECT

How do you feel about the details of your past being the seeds of your future welfare?

∽—PRAYER

Lord, here I am. I bring You my confusion and my anger. Thank You for remembering my fragile frame and for wanting honesty more than right-sounding words. Amen.

HEAR HIS HEART

Therefore, since we have a great high priest who has gone through the heavens, Jesus the Son of God, let us hold firmly to the faith we profess. For we do not have a high priest who is unable to sympathize with our weaknesses, but we have one who has been tempted in every way, just as we are—yet was without sin. Let us then approach the throne of grace with confidence, so that we may receive mercy and find grace to help us in our time of need (Heb. 4:14–16).

A NEW THING

"See, I am doing a new thing!
Now it springs up; do you not perceive it?
I am making a way in the desert
and streams in the wasteland" (Isa. 43:19).

I hardly know who I am anymore. I don't recognize myself. I've forgotten how it feels to be pain-free," wrote a friend who had been progressively healed of fibromyalgia, a disease that causes muscle and joint pain. She went on to describe the spiritual and emotional crisis she experienced because now she had to completely redefine herself and learn a new way to live. Amazing, isn't it? She had suffered so much pain for years that she wasn't sure how to live without it.

It is the same for our emotional pain. We make a truce with it. We learn to live with it. We let it define our lives. It is so much a part of us that we don't even notice it. When it is gone, or when it begins to lessen, we get disoriented. All the behaviors and all the flesh-patterns that I have thought of as "me" are no longer effective. I'm someone altogether new.

When Moses led the Israelites out of Egypt, they knew nothing but slavery. Although they were free, they still cringed in fear when the unexpected happened. And when the conditions of their freedom got a little rough, they longed for the predictable, familiar "security" of their life in Egypt. They grumbled to Moses, "If only we had died by the LORD's hand in Egypt! There we sat around pots of meat and ate all the food we wanted, but you have brought us out into this desert to starve this entire assembly to death" (Exod. 16:3). They had twisted their journey to life into a death march!

You, too, are being freed from bondage to hurt, unconfessed sin, and painful memories. The journey you're taking may get pretty scary sometimes. But learn from the Israelites, and don't yearn to return to what enslaved you. Don't take the pain of new birth and life and distort it into a picture of death. It's time now to learn the new way of the Spirit, leaving behind the old way of the flesh. Let go of the old and take hold of the new with both hands. God is doing a new thing in you. Now it springs up all around you. Look for it. Expect it. Say yes to it!

⌒—REFLECT

Look around you. What new things is God doing? How do they make you feel? What seems more bearable to you: the old familiar pain or the pain of new birth? What are you risking if you turn back?

⌒—PRAYER

Healer, Restorer, Lord, teach me Your way. Guide me in Your truth. Show me what You are doing. I am an entirely new creation. Amen.

HEAR HIS HEART

Therefore, if anyone is in Christ, he is a new creation; the old has gone, the new has come! All this is from God, who reconciled us to himself through Christ and gave us the ministry of reconciliation: that God was reconciling the world to himself in Christ, not counting men's sins against them. And he has committed to us the message of reconciliation (2 Cor. 5:17–19).

SPIRITUAL ANTIOXIDANTS

Let me live that I may praise you,
and may your laws sustain me (Ps. 119:175).

Wellness is a word that has become part of our vocabulary in recent years. It relates to maintaining health rather than treating illness. It refers to actions and lifestyles that lead to the prevention of illness. In the healing that God is doing in you, wellness will eventually become the focus.

Nothing is more powerful in your spiritual wellness program than praise. It sets the stage for God. "He who sacrifices thank offerings honors me, and he prepares the way so that I may show him the salvation of God" (Ps. 50:23). Remember that *salvation* is a saving, healing, and delivering of every part of you. Every time you choose to praise God rather than dwell on the negative in any given situation, you lay the groundwork for His healing to flow.

Praise is not pretense. Praise is based on the solid truth of who God is. He is bringing healing out of every single circumstance. He has a loving purpose for everything He allows in your life. He has a master plan, and each situation fits perfectly into it.

Praise is a powerful spiritual antioxidant, if you'll allow me to use that image. It destroys spiritual toxins before they have a chance to do damage. Praise changes your focus, fixing your eyes on the Supplier more than on the need. Just try to remain discouraged or hurt in the midst of genuine praise. You can't do it!

Try this experiment. At the first hint of stress, anger, or hurt, start looking at the situation for every positive aspect you can find. Then thank God for whatever He is bringing out of it that you can't see right now. Do this as the situation is in progress, not later in review. You will find that you respond differently to the situation. And the other person may very well respond differently to your response. When praise defines the moment instead of anger or hurt, spiritual toxins find nowhere to attach.

Erin and Josh Shaffer are young parents who recently left Kansas City to follow God's call to be missionaries in Jamaica. I saved one of their newsletters from December 2003 because in it Erin wrote the most honest account of moving from disappointment to praise. Let me share her words with you.

"God is so good," I heard myself saying time and again. And then on one occasion I paused. "That's odd," I thought to myself. "Am I only saying that because things are going the way I want them to go?" Our house had sold in only 50 days, and not only that, we had the privilege of choosing between TWO contracts. Our close friends had had their home on the market for a year before it sold. I found myself wondering if I'd still be exalting God and his "perfect plan" in 11 months if my house was still sitting with no offers. A reason for pause.

And then I went to Jamaica, where the majority of people you talk to, despite the fact that they have no idea how they'll put food on the table tomorrow, praise God anyway and truly believe that He's good. Despite the hunger. Despite the lack of medical aid. Despite the fact that seven of them share a one-room house and sleep together in a queen-size bed. It seemed to me that in Jamaica God is good not because of the circumstances surrounding us, but because He IS. A question of character mostly.

And so as I ponder this reality, the phone beeps. A message from our realtor. Bad news: the buyers want out. THEY WHAT!? What kind of person gives us such a short amount of time to get out, pesters us to leave one of our shelves for them, counters the offer THREE times to negotiate a possession time and date, and then says, "Oh you know what—never mind." I was steaming. We had turned down a perfectly good offer from another couple because this was the more promising of the two. I had spent $600 to change our Christmas tickets because we wouldn't be flying out of Kansas City anymore. I wanted to scream and throw something.

And then it all came together. God is good, not because of our circumstances. God is good because that's WHO HE IS. Not because things are happy for me. Not because we have material things or health or children or jobs. It wasn't really a settling fact immediately. I used the words "freaks" and "jerks" more times than I'd like to admit in the following days. But gradually I began to realize that if I held to the idea that God is good BECAUSE I FEEL GOOD, then the opposite would mean that God is not good if I'm suffering in some way. And that's just not true. God is good all the time.

And so I've been mulling over this fact as it relates to many aspects of my life and recalling verses like, "God is light; in Him there is no darkness at all." And thinking about how shallow I can be, and how my emotions so often rule my thoughts. Our house is NOT sold. Our house has NO current offers. We're moving on the 14th anyway. And God is good.

Got it? *God is good!*

So ask the Father to create a heart of worship and praise in you. Invite Him to fill your mouth with His praise so that your lips overflow with it (see Ps. 71:8; 119:171).

ᕲ—REFLECT

Spend time praising God right now. Ask the Spirit to call your heart back to praise all day so that a steady sound of praise and worship ascends from your heart today.

ᕲ—PRAYER

Lord, make me a praise to You in the earth. Let praise rise from me spontaneously, as my first response to anything that comes my way. All my springs of joy are in You. My praise is the proof of my confidence in You. Amen.

HEAR HIS HEART

For you have been my hope, O Sovereign LORD,
my confidence since my youth.
From birth I have relied on you;
you brought me forth from my mother's womb.
I will ever praise you (Ps. 71:5–6).

❧

WHOLENESS

Do not be wise in your own eyes;
fear the LORD and shun evil.
This will bring health to your body
and nourishment to your bones (Prov. 3:7–8).

You can maintain your spiritual, emotional, mental, and relational health by the daily practice of the spiritual disciplines. Even your physical health can be promoted and enhanced by opening your life to the power and provision of God through these disciplines. Knowing God at progressively deeper and more intimate levels, the Bible says, will add fullness to your days, years to your life, healing to your body, and refreshment to your bones (see Prov. 3:1–8; 4:20–22).

This is not to suggest that physical illness is a punishment or that it indicates a lack of faith. Not at all. But it does state in strong and clear terms that keeping your life open to God results in a flow of power that fills your soul and even affects your body.

What are the spiritual disciplines? Traditionally, they are these five:

- Consistent intake of the Word, digesting it and allowing it to bring life and light into your inner self.

- Living a praying life—a life engaged in ongoing and habitual give-and-take with the Father.

- Fellowship with other believers.

- Fasting as the Lord leads, centering your heart on the sustenance you receive from the spiritual realm.

- Tithing and generosity, a sweet-smelling aroma to God.

Ask the Lord to help you develop a spiritually disciplined life, which is essentially a life made open to God's presence and power and love. It is a life to which God has full access and can move and work in all His healing power to bring wholeness at levels too deep for words. He can strip memories of their power to hurt; He can drain off all the sin-infection. As you engage in the disciplines, He will do the work that He alone can do.

ᐁ—REFLECT

What would you identify as the most life-changing truth God has taught you through this experience with healing prayer? How have you changed as a result of healing prayer?

ᐁ—PRAYER

Almighty God, Creator of heaven and earth, Sustainer of all matter and substance, I believe that Your power works in my mortal body. I believe that the very Spirit that raised Jesus from the dead lives in me. I embrace You and all of Your plan for me. Amen.

HEAR HIS HEART

"Those who live in accordance with the Spirit have their minds set on what the Spirit desires. The mind . . . controlled by the Spirit is life and peace" (Rom. 8:5–6).

CONCLUSION

For this reason, ever since I heard about your faith in the Lord Jesus and your love for all the saints, I have not stopped giving thanks for you, remembering you in my prayers. I keep asking that the God of our Lord Jesus Christ, the glorious Father, may give you the Spirit of wisdom and revelation, so that you may know him better. I pray also that the eyes of your heart may be enlightened in order that you may know the hope to which he has called you, the riches of his glorious inheritance in the saints, and his incomparably great power for us who believe. That power is like the working of his mighty strength, which he exerted in Christ when he raised him from the dead and seated him at his right hand in the heavenly realms, far above all rule and authority, power and dominion, and every title that can be given, not only in the present age but also in the one to come. And God placed all things under his feet and appointed him to be head over everything for the church, which is his body, the fullness of him who fills everything in every way (Eph. 1:15–23).

I have been praying for you, and Ephesians 1:15–23 has been my prayer. I want you to focus with me for a moment on this phrase: "his incomparably great power for us who believe" (v. 19). His power is *for* you. Always for you, never against you. The Spirit of God will have to enlighten the eyes of your heart in order that you may know—know from first-hand experience—this power.

Look at how Paul describes this power that is for you. "That power is like the working of his mighty strength, which he exerted in Christ when he raised him from the dead and seated him at his right hand in the heavenly realms, far above all rule and authority, power and dominion, and every title that can be given, not only in the present age but also in the one to come" (vv. 19–21).

It is the power that overpowers every other power. Nothing can stand against it. And the Lord works on your behalf.

Let me encourage you to keep your heart focused on Him and not be distracted by circumstances around you. When you look at your hurts and your wounds, look at them in the context of His power. Don't feel that you have to force healing. Just let healing come.

May God himself, the God of peace, sanctify you through and through. May your whole spirit, soul and body be kept blameless at the coming of our Lord Jesus Christ. The one who calls you is faithful and he will do it (1 Thess. 5:23–24).

20. Merriam-Webster's Collegiate Dictionary, 11th ed., see "relinquish."

21. Dean, *He Restores My Soul*, 140.

WHEN YOU HURT AND WHEN HE HEALS TEAM

ACQUIRING EDITOR
Elsa Mazon

COPY EDITOR
Wendy Peterson

BACK COVER COPY
Elizabeth Cody Newenhuyse

COVER DESIGN
UDG DesignWorks, Inc.

COVER PHOTO
Steve Gardner/pixelworksstudio.net and Digital Vision

INTERIOR DESIGN
Ragont Design

PRINTING AND BINDING
Versa Press, Inc.

The typeface for the text of this book is
Fournier MT